Good News from Matthew

Volume 1

Volume 1

GOOD NEWS
FROM
MATTHEW

Malcolm O. Tolbert

Broadman Press
Nashville, Tennessee

4213-53 (paperback)
ISBN: 0-8054-1353-7

4281-26 (BRP, Volume 1)
4281-27 (BRP, Volume 2)

Library of Congress Catalog Card Number: 75-2537
Dewey Decimal Classification: 226.2
Printed in the United States of America

Volume 1

CONTENTS

Introduction

In about the year 85 of our era, a Christian leader living in Antioch of Syria began to write a book about the ministry of Jesus.° At that moment he could hardly have imagined the tremendous reach and influence that his book would exert during succeeding centuries.

This man was unconcerned about personal notoriety, for he did not even tell us who he was. Our evidence shows that Christians in the first half of the second century believed that he was Matthew, one of the original apostles. They named his book the Gospel according to Matthew. Most modern scholars, however, believe that he was a Jewish-Christian teacher whose name is unknown to us.

A number of resources were available to him as he began to write. Much of his Gospel is similar to the Gospel according to Mark. Probably he had a copy of it before him. Many passages in Matthew, consisting largely of sayings of Jesus, also have parallels only in Luke. He and Luke probably used a document, since lost to us, containing these sayings. It is possible that Matthew the apostle was the original collector of these sayings. In addition, the author of Matthew was acquainted with narratives about Jesus and teachings from him not included in the other two sources.

What motivated the evangelist to write Matthew? No doubt the primary impulse was his conviction about the meaning of

°The Gospel of Matthew does not tell us anything explicitly about the author or his circumstances. This introduction is based on the best "educated guesses" of New Testament scholars.

the ministry of Jesus. He believed that what had happened in Palestine a few short years previously was the gospel. It was the "good news" that God had acted decisively in Jesus of Nazareth to redeem men.

He was neither historian nor biographer, and we need to understand that. He was not writing a "Life of Jesus." History was important to him, as it is to us. Everything depends upon the truth of the gospel, that is, that Jesus lived, died, and was raised from the dead.

The evangelist, however, was above all a man of faith, proclaiming the saving word of God which mere history and biography cannot reach. Christ died. That is fact. Christ died *for our sins.* That is the saving word whose truth is known alone to people who have responded to it.

The evangelist was probably a Jew by birth, concerned with his own people. He was especially disturbed by the failure of Jews to recognize that Jesus was the fulfillment of God's promises, the answer to their own hopes and expectations. Much of his Gospel was written to show that the life, death, and resurrection of Jesus were the climax of God's redemptive activity described in the old Testament.

The Jewish people were looking for a messiah, a king, to liberate them and reestablish the rule of David over a new and glorious kingdom of the end-time. One of Matthew's major points is that Jesus is that messianic king.

The evangelist was also interested in the church. He was probably a teacher, engaged in the study of gospel materials with other church leaders. His is the only Gospel in which the word *church* is found. He is the only writer who deals with the problem of church discipline (Matt. 18:15-20).

Furthermore, to the extent that it was possible, the evangelist organized his materials so that they would be easy for church leaders to use in teaching the gospel to new Christians. He grouped his materials about the public ministry of Jesus into five major sections, each of which has a dominant theme. Each of these sections consists of two parts. The first part is largely narrative in character, and the second is made up primarily of sayings of Jesus. These sections conclude with the statements found at 7:28; 11:1; 13:53; 19:1; and 26:1. If you look at these statements, you will notice how similar they are to one another.

In addition to the five major sections into which the ministry of Jesus is divided, you will find two other important sections in Matthew. The Gospel begins with the birth and infancy narratives found in chapters 1 and 2. It ends with the narratives of the crucifixion and resurrection, which begin at 26:2. A general outline of Matthew would look like the following:

Prologue: The Birth and Infancy Narratives - Matthew 1—2
I. Discipleship - Matthew 3—7
    A. Narrative: the beginning of Jesus' ministry—Matthew 3—4
    B. Discourse: the Sermon on the Mount—Matthew 5—7
II. Apostleship - Matthew 8—10
    A. Narrative: Jesus' healing and teaching ministry—Matthew 8:1 to 9:34
    B. Discourse: the mission of the apostles—Matthew 9:35 to 10:42
III. The Hidden Revelation - Matthew 11:1 to 13:52
    A. Narrative: opposition to Jesus—Matthew 11—12
    B. Discourse: the hidden teaching in parables—Matthew 13:1-52
IV. The Church - Matthew 13:53 to 18:35
    A. Narrative: the suffering of the Messiah—Matthew 13:53 to 17:23
    B. Discourse: church administration—Matthew 17:24 to 18:35
V. The Judgment - Matthew 19—25
    A. Narrative: controversies in Jerusalem—Matthew 19—22
    B. Discourse: condemnation of the religious leaders

Foreword

We asked Dr. Tolbert to do an exposition of Matthew that would bring out its meaning and message for today. We wanted a book for Bible students rather than scholars. This commentary, therefore, does not deal extensively with technical and critical problems. It will be especially useful to the Sunday School teacher and preacher who are attempting to interpret the Gospel for people as they live in today's world.

Although this is not a verse-by-verse treatment of the Gospel, it does not ignore any verses. The two volumes of *Good News from Matthew* are divided into twenty-three chapters. Each chapter has several sections, each one dealing with a group of verses, consecutively through the Gospel. A brief, indented paragraph opens each section to summarize its content. Then the interpretation of the passage is presented under two or more subheads. Thus, the teachings of Matthew are readily available to the reader with an open Bible.

Dr. Tolbert is a capable New Testament scholar. He has an earned doctorate, was a teaching missionary in Brazil for nine years, and has been teaching New Testament and Greek at New Orleans Baptist Seminary since 1961. This is his fourth book, plus his interpretation of "Luke" in *The Broadman Bible Commentary*. He is thoroughly acquainted with the literature on Matthew.

THE EDITORS

1.
Son of David

1:1 to 2:23

1. Jesus, the Fulfillment of Jewish Expectations (Matt. 1: 1-17)

Jewish people considered themselves the heirs of the promise and covenant made with Abraham. They also believed that a descendant of David would be their national deliverer. Matthew taught that those hopes are fulfilled in Jesus.

1. The opening verse. Matthew gives to the central figure of his Gospel the title "Jesus Christ, the son of David, the son of Abraham." This verse may very well have been intended as an introduction to the whole Gospel rather than just to the genealogy.

It meant far more to the Jewish audience of the first century than it does to the casual reader of the New Testament today. Jesus is presented as much more than a descendant of both Abraham and David. Others could claim with him this noble lineage. He was that special son of Abraham and David in whom all the history of God's dealing with his people came to a climax and in whom all their hopes and expectations were fulfilled.

2. His name. Jesus is a translation of the Greek equivalent of the Hebrew *Joshua.* It meant "Jahweh (the Lord) saves" or "Jahweh is salvation." Joshua was one of the most famous heroes of Israel's past. Consequently his was a popular name among Jews of Jesus' own time, given to their sons by Jewish parents as a testimony of their faith in God.

Christ is *Christos* in Greek, *Mashiah* (Messiah) in Hebrew. Both

11

terms meant "anointed one," a title that had come to be used to designate the hoped-for deliverer of the end-time. The Christ (Messiah) was expected to throw off foreign rule, judge his people, establish a kingdom of righteousness, and attract the nations from the ends of the earth to see his glory. Matthew affirms that Jesus is this Messiah. In his Gospel, he will correct false messianic expectations and show Israel that her promised King had established a rule of unlimited dimensions and of glorious hope, which transcended her narrow, nationalistic, and political conceptions.

3. The genealogy. It is constructed so as to call attention to its pivotal points, as Matthew himself shows (see 1:17). These pivotal points are Abraham, David, the deportation to Babylon, and the birth of Jesus, to which it all leads. Evidently Matthew intended the genealogy to have three sections, consisting of fourteen generations each. If you count the names in the last section, however, you will find but thirteen. Perhaps Matthew included Mary to round out the number. You will also notice that Jesus is presented by Matthew as a descendant of kings. His is a royal lineage as befits the greatest King of them all.

4. Abraham, the father of the Jewish people. The promise and the covenant had been given to Abraham. The Jewish people believed that their present relationship with God depended on their physical relationship to their great ancestor. Their hope for the future was also tied to their descent from him. Abraham was the model of virtue, obedience, and faith whom God had rewarded, they believed, by making him his friend. They believed that God would receive the sons of Abraham into his presence out of consideration for their ancestor, his greatest servant. But Matthew taught that God's promises to Abraham would be fulfilled through men's relationship to Jesus.

5. David. Israel's greatest king, the outstanding ruler of her glory days, was David. Moreover, God through Nathan had promised that a descendant of David would rule over his people forever (2 Sam. 7:12-16).

6. The deportation into Babylon. The exile apparently frustrated this promise of God. Israel was no longer ruled by a son of David but by hated foreign oppressors. This period of foreign rule was broken for about a century by a national resurgence under the Hasmonean rulers after the Maccabean revolt. But these Hasmoneans, although Jews, were not descendants of David. Their rule, therefore, was resented by the more orthodox of Jewish people. This brief period of independence had come to an end with the arrival of the Romans in 63 B.C.

About this time, triggered apparently by the Roman rule, some Jews began to reinterpret the ancient promise to David. A deliverer would arise, a son of David, who would throw off the Roman yoke and reestablish the Davidic dynasty in Jerusalem. The term, son of David, first used in the Psalms of Solomon (about 50 B.C.), became another title for the Messiah. So you see what Matthew meant when he applied it to Jesus.

7. The women in the genealogy. The circumstances by which the women in the genealogy became involved in Israel's royal line were extremely unusual. Tamar (1:3) was wife of Er, Judah's oldest son. After her husband's death, she presented herself to Judah disguised as a prostitute. Her sons, Perez and Zerah, were the products of this deceptive relationship.

Rahab (1:5) is usually identified as the harlot of Jericho, who saved the spies put into Jericho by Joshua. This identification, however, is not certain. Ruth (1:5) was a Moabite, a foreigner. The wife of Uriah (1:6) was Bathsheba. David exploited her sexually and then sent Uriah into battle to be slain. The presence of these women in the genealogy shows in a dramatic way how God used all kinds of people in his redemptive work.

8. Joseph and Jesus. In verse 16, Matthew describes Joseph's relationship to Jesus. You should know that there are some different readings of this verse in the ancient manuscripts. One of them describes Joseph as the father of Jesus. This is not thought to be the correct text. At any rate, the story of Jesus' birth makes it clear that Matthew did not teach that Joseph was the real father of Jesus. He was, however, his legal father. In Matthew's eyes, his relationship was such as to satisfy the Jewish belief that the Messiah would be David's descendant.

II. The Unexpected Jesus (Matt. 1:18-25)

Matthew's view of Jesus went far beyond current Jewish expectations. He shows this in what he taught about (1) the manner of his birth, (2) the nature of his person, and (3) the character of his mission.

1. The manner of his birth.   Mary became pregnant during her betrothal to Joseph. Betrothal was the stage that preceded marriage. But in Jewish betrothal the woman was expected to display the same faithfulness as she would later in marriage. Infidelity during betrothal was regarded as adultery and was punishable under the law prohibiting such actions.

Joseph concluded that Mary had been unfaithful to him. He was a just man, which probably means he was faithful to the law. The only course open to him was divorce. Of course, the law even sanctioned the harsh penalty of death by stoning. But Joseph's justice was tempered with mercy. To avoid open scandal, he resolved to divorce Mary privately before the minimum number of witnesses. He was deterred from executing his plans by a message from God revealing the true origin of Jesus.

The emphasis for Matthew, and Luke also, is on the teaching that Jesus was conceived by the Holy Spirit rather than on the virginity of Mary. That Jesus is God's Son is a teaching which runs through the New Testament. The virgin birth is mentioned only in the opening verses of Matthew and Luke.

God worked a miracle in Mary, a miracle of creation, that brought into being a new humanity. It was a miracle comparable to the creation miracle of the beginning.

2. The nature of his person.   Matthew explains that Jesus was to bear his name for a special reason. He makes a claim for Jesus that went far beyond anything the Jews expected. They believed that the Messiah would be a man used by the Lord (Jahweh) to save his people. But Matthew declares that Jesus is none other than the Lord who saves.

He is Immanuel, God with us (1:23). This is set forth in the first of many quotations from the Old Testament found in Matthew. All the Gospel writers emphasize the fulfillment of prophecy in the life of Jesus, but Matthew stresses this more than the others. The difference in Matthew is one of degree. The central conviction of the gospel is the belief that in Jesus, God himself appeared among men, lived with them, vulnerable to their hurts and diseases, and died out of love for them.

Matthew's quotation of Isaiah 7:14 (Matt. 1:23) is taken from the Septuagint, the Greek translation of Old Testament writings. "Young woman" is probably the best translation of the much debated term, if one is using the Hebrew text. Even the Greek word of the Septuagint, *parthenos,* does not necessarily mean "virgin" in the English sense. But without any doubt, Matthew teaches that Mary was a virgin in the strictest sense until Jesus was born.

Joseph did not "know her," that is, he did not have sexual relations with her before Jesus' birth. The text implies that this changed after that. Indeed the clear evidence of the New Testament is that Joseph and Mary had several children (see Matt. 12:46; Mark 6:3).

3. *The nature of his mission.*   The Jews expected a Messiah who would save them from foreign domination and who would reestablish the Davidic rule in Jerusalem. But Matthew taught that in Jesus, God had appeared to save them from their sins (1:21).

Man's greatest need is not for a new political or economic order. His primary problem is his sin. He is alienated from God, bearing the burden of this guilt and loneliness, facing a frightening future. He needs to be liberated from the tyranny of his sins, reconciled to God, and given a hope that transcends the circumstances of this life.

III. Bethlehem, Birthplace of the King (Matt. 2:1-12)

Jesus, born in Bethlehem in fulfillment of a prophecy found in Micah 5:2, is worshiped by foreigners and feared by Herod.

1. *The Wise Men.* The story of the visit of the Wise Men has captured the imagination of people through the ages. They are called magi. This is the transliteration of the Greek word. Elsewhere in the New Testament it is used in a bad sense (e.g. Acts 13:6) to mean magician.

These Wise Men were evidently astrologers who had interpreted the appearing of a new star in the heavens as the portent of an unusual event, namely, the birth of the long-awaited messianic Jewish King. Matthew's account implies that these men, possibly from Persia, were aware of Jewish thought.

The learned men from the East naturally went to Jerusalem, the Jewish capital, to make their inquiries. The idea that they were led all the way by the star is, therefore, an assumption unwarranted by the text. In Jerusalem they learned that Bethlehem was to be the birthplace of the King. This was confirmed by the apparent reappearance of the star over that city. English translations generally tell us that they "worshiped" him. This probably should be understood as "they paid him homage" in a way that would befit such a royal person. They offered him gifts in keeping with the occasion—gold, frankincense, and myrrh. Frankincense was a fragrant gum resin which was ground into powder and burned, emitting a blossomlike odor. Myrrh was also a fragrant resin. It was used in sacred anointing oil and in perfume for beauty treatment and for scenting clothes.

Is Matthew drawing a contrast between the openness and receptivity of the foreign visitors and the blindness of Jesus' own people? Perhaps so.

2. *Herod, the king.* Herod the Great was the man who ruled

the Jews under the Romans (40-4 B.C.). He was in a sense a usurper of the throne. He was an Idumean, a descendant of the people who had been forced to become Jews by the Hasmonean John Hyrcanus (Jewish ruler 135-105 B.C.). Herod was, thus, hated and despised by large segments of the Jewish people. In many ways, he was an able administrator. Among other achievements, he initiated the building of the Temple in which Jesus and his contemporaries worshiped. But he was also cruel, despotic, and paranoid. He even caused several of his sons and his most loved wife, Mariamne, a Hasmonean princess, to be executed.

The news of the possible birth of a legitimate rival to the throne aroused all of Herod's fears. Jesus is described to him by the magi as a "born king of the Jews," that is, a legitimate heir to the throne. This was in contrast to Herod who had gained the throne through adroit political maneuvering and held it because he was backed by the conqueror's power.

From both Luke and Matthew we learn that Jesus was born while Herod the Great still ruled the Jews. This means that his birth can be dated no later than 4 B.C.

3. *The fulfillment of prophecy.* Perhaps Matthew's major interest was the fulfillment of the prophecy cited in 2:6. Both Luke and Matthew agree that Jesus was born in Bethlehem. But their accounts show they had completely different interests. Luke emphasized the humble surroundings of Jesus' birth. The first people to become aware of the enormous event are simple shepherds. Matthew was more concerned about circumstances which show that Jesus was Israel's long-awaited king whose coming was in keeping with the data gleaned from the Old Testament.

Perhaps one point should be clarified here. Early Christians did not come to the conviction that Jesus was the Messiah, God's Son, by their study of the Old Testament. They did not move from prophecy to fulfillment originally. They first came to the conviction that Jesus was the Messiah in the light especially of the resurrection. But they also had another conviction. The God of the Old Testament was also the God and Father of Jesus Christ. This meant that there must be coherence between what God had done in the past and what he had done in Jesus. They searched the Old Testament from this perspective and found here, there, and yonder statements which in their minds pointed indubitably to Christ.

IV. Escape from Deadly Peril (Matt. 2:13-23)

Like their ancestors of old, Joseph and Mary are forced by circumstances in Palestine to flee to Egypt with their newborn child.

1. The flight to Egypt. The description of Herod's savage attempts to eliminate a possible rival to the Jewish throne fits well what we know of his brutality. A man who had slain his own sons would not hesitate to kill another child who might be considered by the Jews to be their legitimate ruler.

Because the Wise Men returned to their homeland without reporting to him, Herod was foiled in his crafty scheme to learn the identity of the child. This forced him to undertake drastic measures to achieve his aims. He ordered the slaughter of all children in Bethlehem up to two years of age. This action was based on information furnished to him by the Wise Men about the date of the star's appearing. Matthew saw the slaughter of the infants as a fulfillment of an Old Testament passage (Jer. 31:15). If you study these passages in their context, you will find that they had a different meaning to their contemporaries than that given by the New Testament writer. This one, for example, was evoked by the desolation of Judea and the captivity of her people by the Babylonians.

Herod's attempts to destroy the newborn king were frustrated by God's intervention. Joseph had a vision in which he was commanded to get up at that very moment to take Mary and the child to Egypt. Haste was of the essence if he was to escape Herod's clutches.

Once again this flight to Egypt is related to an Old Testament passage (v. 15; cf. Hos. 11:1). In the Old Testament context, the reference was to the liberation of God's people from their slavery in Egypt. But New Testament writers make much of the idea that many of Israel's experiences were recapitulated in the life of Jesus.

There is a lesson to be learned from this incident. God does not always use the spectacular, powerful method to achieve his ends. The paradox is that God's Son is saved by ignominious flight. This should cause us to be careful about how we assess God's actions. We generally link him with the spectacular, the miraculous. But his actions are often hidden actions, undiscerned by people who have fixed ideas about what he must do and how he must do it.

2. The return to Palestine.   The death of Herod (4 B.C.) made it possible for Joseph and his family to return to their native land. But they decided not to settle in Judea because Archelaus ruled that region (4 B.C.—A.D. 6) after the death of his father. Archelaus had all the weaknesses and sins of his father with none of his strengths. He was deposed by the Romans in A.D. 6 because his harsh and cruel actions created so many problems in the territory.

Joseph and Mary settled with Jesus in Nazareth in the region of Galilee. This region had been given to Herod Antipas by the Romans when his father died. Antipas was the ruler of Galilee throughout the life of Jesus.

Verse 23 contains a problem that is insoluble on the basis of our present data. Nazareth is mentioned nowhere in the Old Testament. The word translated Nazarene is *Nazaraios,* a word whose significance is unknown. One guess is that it is related to a word meaning "shoot" (*nezer*) found in Isaiah 11:1. There are other conjectures, but we must conclude that we simply do not know what Matthew had in mind when he wrote verse 23.

2.
My Beloved Son

3:1 to 4:22

I. The Appearance of John the Baptist (Matt. 3:1-10)

The gospel story begins with the appearance of John in the uninhabited region near the Jordan River and his call for repentance. He rejects Jewish leaders because their desire for baptism does not represent a real turning from their sins.

1. The person of John the Baptist. We have a lot of unanswered questions about John. He is indeed a figure enveloped in mystery. What was his background and preparation for ministry? Why did he take such a task upon himself? What are the antecedents of his baptism? How did he understand his role? Just what was his relationship to Jesus? We have no definitive answers to these questions.

The reason the Gospel writers did not tell us more is simple. They were not interested in his biography. His appearance was the most important thing. According to a generally held tenet of Jewish messianic belief, Elijah the prophet would return as the forerunner of the Messiah (Mal. 4:5). Early Christians believed that John fulfilled that expectation.

This is why the writers gave a description of his attire. Like Elijah of old, "he wore a garment of haircloth, with a girdle of leather about his loins" (2 Kings 1:8). Also, he ate the food available to him in that uninhabited region. The appearance of the forerunner was the signal that the Messiah was about to come. The gospel story proper begins at this point.

2. *The message of John the Baptist.* The theme of John's preaching is succinctly stated: "Repent." Repentance means more than being sorry for sins. The Greek word means to change one's mind. Of course, this is involved. The basic meaning of the word, however, is found in its Old Testament antecedents. Repentance means a turning, a decisive change of direction in life. John called on people to turn from their sins and to turn toward God.

Repentance is primarily a relational word. Man in sin is out of relation with God. The primary sin problem is not that man has broken this rule or that. It is that he has rejected God's right to rule over his life. His primary need is to be in right relation with his God. Even good people, you see, need to repent.

The urgency of John's call for people to get right with God is contained in the declaration "for the kingdom of heaven is at hand." "Kingdom of heaven" is found only in Matthew (32 times). Elsewhere it is the "kingdom of God" (also 4 times in Matthew), which means the same thing. The kingdom of God is the rule or reign of God. It should not be identified with a territory or a culture. It cannot be promoted or extended by man. It can only be proclaimed, as John does here and as Jesus does subsequently.

God is in fact king at all times and in all places. But there are many people who do not recognize him as king and who do not accept his rule over their lives. This was true in John's day as it is in ours.

John affirmed that God was about to demonstrate his kingly rule in a new and decisive way. The Messiah, God's anointed one, was about to appear as the bearer of God's kingly power. He would demonstrate it in salvation and judgment. This seems to be what John had in mind.

3. *The baptism of John.* Whence came John's baptism? What are its antecedents? Once again there are no assured answers. We know that Jews baptized proselytes. But the earliest concrete evidence for this practice is later than John. There is a possibility that the practice antedates him and gave him this concrete symbol for turning from sin to God. John's baptism was different, however, in that he baptized Jews and not Gentiles.

The Essene community at Qumran practiced baptisms. These, however, were purification rites that were repeated frequently. The people who came to John, on the other hand, were baptized only once.

John's baptism was the public expression of the personal decision for God. It was to be followed by a repentant life, that is, a life lived under God's rule. John said: "I baptize you with water for repentance" (3:11).

While baptism could be a public act of repentance, it did not itself bring about repentance. This is seen clearly in John's rejection of the Pharisees and Sadducees who came to be baptized by him. The Pharisees constituted an important Jewish sect. They magnified that body of oral traditions designed to show Jews how to keep the law. These oral traditions had been developing for a long time. The Sadducees, another Jewish sect, were primarily a priestly party whose power base was the Temple and the Sanhedrin. They accepted only the Pentateuch (the first five books of the Old Testament), and rejected many Pharisaic beliefs, including the oral tradition, angels, and the resurrection.

We do not know how John reached his judgment about the motives of the Jewish leaders. He discerned, however, that they were simply trying to save themselves from the wrath of the Messiah. Fear was their motive. They were like a bunch of snakes fleeing from a fire raging across a field.

This raises a question about the legitimacy of fear of personal destruction as a reason for turning to God. At least we can say that it is not the highest motive. Men should turn toward God because of who he is and because they find the true purpose of life in serving and loving him.

"Bear fruit that befits repentance," John thundered at the would-be candidates for baptism. Luke gives concrete examples of this fruit (Luke 3:10 ff.). Matthew does not elaborate. The fruit is the kind of life which shows that a decisive change in direction has taken place.

Nor were the leaders to find comfort in their claims to a relationship to God based on race. Being physical descendants of Abraham was not enough. Character would be the test— character manifested by the fruit of a life lived by God's purpose. The farmer cut down the tree which did not produce good, that is, useful, edible fruits. Just so would the descendants of Abraham who did not manifest the fruits of a repentant life suffer the wrath of God.

II. The Baptism of Jesus (Matt. 3:11-16)

> John predicts the coming of a mightier one who will baptize with the Holy Spirit and fire. Jesus then comes to the Jordan to be baptized by John.

1. The mightier one.   The relationship between John and Jesus was evidently a problem for the early church. Some people got the notion that John himself was the Messiah. We have evidence of a John the Baptist movement that continued after the death of the baptizer and that was probably a rival to Christianity. Its followers may have claimed that John was superior to Jesus.

In all the Gospels, the witness of John to his own role is given. His task is a subordinate one. He is not the Messiah. He is not the bearer of God's kingly rule. That role is to be filled by one mightier than he.

The contrast between the two baptisms is an indication of the contrast between John and the Coming One. John baptizes with water, but he who is coming will baptize with the Holy Spirit and fire.

For centuries the voice of prophecy had been stilled among the Jews. The Spirit no longer filled men so that they could give a direct message from God. The will of God could be known only by searching the Scriptures. But Jewish people believed that

with the coming of the Messiah, the Spirit would be poured out
on men again (cf. Joel 2:28 ff.). Once again men would receive
a direct message from God. In the messianic age, however, the
gift of prophecy would not be limited to a few. As Joel had said,
the Spirit would be poured out "upon all flesh."

To say that the coming one would baptize with the Holy Spirit
was to say that he was the Messiah. John was declaring that the
messianic age was about to begin.

We may note at this point a common, fallacious tenet of Pen-
tecostal theology. I refer to the tendency to separate the conversion
experience from Spirit baptism. The function of the Messiah in
his coming was to baptize with the Spirit. This was to be his
ministry. In Christian theology in the New Testament, therefore,
the coming of Jesus to a person, that is, his conversion, is specifically evidenced by the giving of the Spirit.

There is a great deal of discussion over the meaning of fire
in 3:11. Mark has only the Holy Spirit in the parallel passage
(cf. Mark 1:8). Some argue that fire is a symbol of the Holy Spirit
which emphasizes the Spirit's cleansing, purifying effect on God's
people.

Others, however, argue that John refers here to the two-fold
work of the Messiah. He will pour God's Spirit out on the repentant. He will be the agent of God's wrath toward the rebellious.
Fire, from this point of view, signifies the destroying wrath of
God.

The two roles of the Messiah as Savior and Judge are delineated
in verse 12. Wheat represents the people who have turned to
God. Chaff represents the people who have rejected the rule of
God. The metaphor, of course, was taken from an agricultural
activity perenially seen across the land at the time of the wheat
harvest.

2. Why was Jesus baptized?   The story shows that John pro-
tested Jesus' request to be baptized. He needed the baptism that
Jesus could give, that is, baptism with the Spirit. Why would

the Messiah desire John's water baptism, which represented a turning from sin?

We are in touch here with one of the vexing questions of New Testament study. Indeed, it has been a problem for Christians from the very beginning. One of the basic Christian beliefs about Jesus is that he was free from sin and, therefore, not an object of John's primary message.

Jesus explained it thus: "It is fitting for us to fulfill all righteousness." Jesus evidently understood that God willed his baptism. To do what God wills is the fulfillment of righteousness. Righteousness is more a positive than a negative concept. We generally think of goodness in a negative kind of way. A good person does not violate certain moral standards. But this negative aspect of Jesus' righteousness is little emphasized in the New Testament. His righteousness was translated into loving service of God—being and doing exactly what God intended.

But Jesus' statement does not resolve the problem. Why did he believe that God wanted him to come to a baptism that was for sinners? We cannot answer the question fully. But we can make some statements about it.

Jesus came to his baptism with the consciousness that he was the Messiah. It marked the beginning of his messianic ministry and is so understood by the Gospel writers. In it Jesus was dedicating himself to his messianic vocation. It was in a real sense his ordination as the Messiah.

The Messiah in Jewish thought was to be identified with his people. The Messiah's people were those who had been prepared by John—who had turned to God from their sins and were expectantly awaiting the bearer of their salvation. How could he better express his identification with them than by becoming one with them through submission to John's baptism?

In his baptism, therefore, Jesus was initiating his ministry as Messiah, ready to do whatever God wanted him to do. In his baptism he was also identifying himself with his people, ready to accept their lot and participate in their rejection and suffering.

3. The voice from heaven.   At the baptism the Spirit descended on Jesus "like a dove." This metaphor is probably intended to remind us of Genesis 1:2, which says that the Spirit of God was moving or hovering over the unformed universe. There is no place in the Old Testament, however, where the dove is a symbol of the Spirit. Probably the point in the reference is that Jesus is here equipped for his messianic role of baptizing with the Spirit.

The heavenly statement is a combination of two passages from the Old Testament. The first is found in Psalm 2:7. This psalm had come to be viewed as messianic in certain Jewish circles. They took it to describe the coronation of the King Messiah. "With whom I am well pleased" probably refers to the phrase in Isaiah 42:1: "my chosen in whom my soul delights." This is found in one of the Servant passages of Isaiah. Thus, we find two Old Testament concepts brought together—King Messiah and Suffering Servant. This may be taken to indicate that Jesus is the Messiah but that his role is not that of a national conquering hero. Rather, this is a Messiah whose ministry involves that of being the Suffering Servant of the Lord. The unlikely combination of these two concepts represents Jesus' unique understanding of his own role.

III. The Temptations of Jesus (Matt. 4:1-11)

> Like the Israelites of old, God's Son faces temptation in an uninhabited region. Unlike them, his faith in God does not waver. In the temptations, he rejects popular notions of the Messiah's work and methods.

1. Jesus' temptations and Israel's.   The relationship between the temptation of Jesus and the experience of Israelites during the time of Moses is clearly seen. The place is the wilderness, the uninhabited region west of the Dead Sea and near the Jordan where Jesus was baptized. In a similar region the faith of the Israelites was tested by difficult experiences. Indeed, as a result of this episode of Israel's history, the desert or wilderness assumed a theological significance as the place of testing.

The time of testing is forty days and nights. This reminds us also of the forty years duration of the wilderness sojourn. It further reminds us of the experience of Elijah (1 Kings 19:8).

Jesus' temptations showed striking similarities to Israel's. The lack of food (cf. Ex. 16), the demand for a spectacular demonstration of God's power (cf. Ex. 17:1-7, especially v. 7), and the worship of the devil (Ex. 32:1-23) are all paralleled in the Old Testament narrative.

Furthermore, the replies to the temptations all are taken from Deuteronomy, that is from the time of the wilderness wandering. They were admonitions from God intended to keep his people from succumbing to temptations. Jesus used these words from God to defeat the devil.

The contrast between Jesus' experience and Israel's however, is apparent. The Israelites of old had been unequal to the testing in the desert. They had lost faith in God, had made presumptuous demands on him, had slipped into idolatry. But this strong Son of God remained faithful against all these temptations during his forty-day trial in the desert.

2. The significance of the temptations. It is interesting that the stress of temptation followed on the heels of the exalted experience of baptism. Jesus had committed himself to God, had received confirmation of his vocation from the heavenly voice, and had received the Spirit. We might think that this "mountaintop experience" would have insulated him from the power of temptations. But not so. Indeed, the opposite is so often true in human experience. The moment of exultation is many times succeeded by a period of depression and doubt.

Moreover, there was a major question facing Jesus. He had embraced his vocation as Messiah. But he still had to decide what kind of Messiah he would be.

This was not an easy choice, given the popular notions entertained by the Jewish people. They wanted a national deliverer to throw off Roman domination. They certainly did not expect a Messiah who would take the path of the Suffering Servant, be humiliated by rejection, and finally die on a cross. If Jesus was to fulfill his role as the people's redeemer through suffering, he had to resist tremendous pressures which would arise even from his own followers. That is exactly what he did in his victory over his temptations.

3. The interpretation of the temptations. "If you are the Son of God"—there is the insidious, crafty, opening wedge. Surely, God's Son should not be in this condition of near starvation in a world that God himself created. The world always assumes that the possession of power implies its use, especially for the benefit of the one who possesses it.

It is the same kind of temptation to which children of God are constantly susceptible. Why do I suffer in this way, since I am a believer in God? Why would he allow his children to endure deprivation, hunger, and disease, at the same time allowing the unjust and ungodly to enjoy good health and prosperity? It is enough to cause one to doubt that he is God's child—or perhaps that there is a God at all. "Command these stones to become loaves of bread." That seems to be such a logical use of power. There were many stones lying around but no bread. If we could, would we not change them to bread in similar circumstances?

But Jesus did not base his faith in God on the physical circumstances of his life. God had taught a great lesson to the Israelites in the wilderness. Man's total existence depends on the word of God and not on the material necessities of life. God's word had come to him: "This is my beloved Son." Jesus would depend on that affirmation rather than on the ready supply of provisions to meet his physical needs.

So God's children often have to depend on the word that has come to them when all circumstances seem to contradict that word. We are his children. We belong to him. His word has come to us in the events of the gospel—in Christ's death and resurrection.

Our existence depends on that word rather than on the amount of food in the cupboard or money in the bank.

The second temptation was for Jesus to do the spectacular to prove his relationship to God and get people to believe that he was the Messiah.

What could be more spectacular than a plunge from the pinnacle of the Temple? We do not know with assurance what the pinnacle was. Most guess that it was the southeast wall where there was a sheer drop into the Kidron Valley. Could Jesus not expect a miracle from God? By leaping would he not be demonstrating the kind of faith to which God responds? The devil even quoted Scripture to prove that this kind of spectacular "seed-faith" would cause God to do what he had already said he would do. This should put us on guard against the similar use of Scripture.

The answer is no! The children of Israel had put God to such a test long ago, and he had condemned them for it (cf. Deut. 6:16). Man is not to back God in a corner. That is not faith; it is presumption. God must always be free to act on his own terms and not on terms laid down by man. "You shall not tempt [i.e., put to the test] the Lord your God."

The greatest faith of all is not miracle-working faith. It is rather the trust and confidence of the great servants of God who in the midst of suffering and weakness demand no miracles at all.

The third temptation involves the offer of world dominion. This indeed was the dream of many of Jesus' people. And they had their ideas about how it would come about. Some believed that God would intervene directly through his Messiah and usher in the longed-for time of the end. Still others (the zealots) believed that God's Messiah would lead his people in a war of national liberation and conquest.

The idolatry of the Israelites in building the calf and worshiping it in the desert is obvious and blatant. God had this and similar pagan relapses in mind when he had commanded the people to fear and serve God alone (Deut. 6:13).

But there is a subtler kind of idolatry. And it is often masked under the cloak of religion. That was the sin of the zealots. They claimed to be totally dedicated to God but their methods and goals were satanic. Jesus refused to allow himself to be pressured into taking the same route. He would worship God by surrendering his life to be his servant. He would not grasp for worldly power by the evil methods. To do so would be to worship the devil.

We have so identified worship with what we do at eleven o'clock on Sunday morning that we fail to understand the broader significance of the term. We forget that Paul called for the giving of our total selves to God as our worship (Rom. 12:1-2). We can hardly call worship what is done during that Sunday morning hour if our whole approach to life and its goals is not an expression of service to God. We are worshiping the devil if we live by his methods, no matter what we do on Sunday at church.

IV. The Beginning of the Galilean Ministry (Matt. 4:12-22)

> After the arrest of John the Baptist, Jesus goes to Galilee and begins preaching the same message that John proclaimed. He calls the first disciples.

1. *The arrest of John.*   The arrest of John the Baptist by Herod Antipas, Herod the Great's son who ruled Galilee and Perea under the Romans, seems to have been the occasion for Jesus to leave the region of the Baptist's ministry to go to Galilee. Capernaum, a town on the Sea of Galilee, was the center of his ministry there. We may guess that his withdrawal from the Judean wilderness was caused by the conditions that had brought about John's arrest.

The arrest of John, which of course ended in his execution, brought an end to his ministry. Apparently this was the signal for Jesus to begin his.

2. *The call of the first disciples.*   Early in the ministry Jesus called the first four of that special group of disciples whom we often call the twelve apostles. This incident is instructive. First of all, the call was to follow Jesus. We know in retrospect what

those early fishermen hardly perceived at that moment. The call to follow Jesus involved identification with him, not only in his victories and popularity but also in his rejection and humiliation. It meant to walk the way that led to the cross.

The key to the meaning of the word *disciple* is found here. It is often said that disciple means "learner." And that is the general meaning of the Greek word. But what it means to be a disciple of Jesus must be set in the context of the gospel. It means to be a follower of Jesus. This meaning with its implications will be elaborated elsewhere in the Gospel.

But one meaning becomes clear even at this initial moment. The call to follow Jesus is a call to make a radical break with the old life. For Peter, Andrew, James, and John, it meant that they left nets, boats, and father. The text emphasizes that this was done immediately. These men would continue to be fishermen but in a new and higher sense. The place of their fishing would no longer be the waters of Galilee but the towns and villages of the land. No longer would their purpose in life be to capture fish but to attract men to join them in discipleship.

3.
Blessed Are You

4:23 to 5:16

I. Jesus' Ministry in Galilee (Matt. 4:23 to 5:1)

Jesus conducts a great ministry of teaching, preaching, and healing in Galilee. As a result great crowds from Galilee and the surrounding regions flock to him.

1. The region of his ministry.   Jesus' ministry unfolded initially in the territory which was often called "Galilee of the Gentiles" (see 4:15) because it was inhabited by a mixed population. Galilee had been a part of the Northern Kingdom that resulted from a partition of Israel following the reign of Solomon. At one time or another it had been ruled by Assyrians, Babylonians, Persians, Greeks, Egyptians, and Syrians. So foreign influence was strong in the region.

Although Jesus evidently confined his activities to Galilee at this time, he attracted great crowds from Syria to the north, from the Jewish province of Judea to the south, from Perea beyond the Jordan, and from Decapolis. The Decapolis consisted of Gentile cities, centers of Greek culture, located for the most part east of the Jordan.

2. Aspects of his ministry.   Matthew tells us that Jesus taught, proclaimed the good news of God's rule, and healed the sick. These were three interrelated functions, all directed toward the same end. His preaching consisted of the proclamation that God's kingly power was breaking into the realm of human history in a new and crucial way. Because of this, men were called on to repent and accept his salvation.

His healing was a revelation that Jesus himself possessed this kingly power. He demonstrated it by his ascendancy over the forces that overpower and afflict men. But he wanted men to see the deeper meaning of his miracles. He had the power to deal with their most critical needs by delivering them from the power of sin.

We have many examples of Jesus' teaching in the Gospels. He had to deal with the questions, problems, and issues raised by his proclamation of the kingship of God. In the synagogues, his teaching was likely an exposition of the passage read in the service.

3. Teaching in the synagogues. Synagogues had arisen among the Jewish people to provide places for worship and study. Many scholars trace their origin to the time of the Exile when the people were separated from their homeland and denied the possibility of worship in the Temple.

Each sabbath people gathered in the synagogues to pray, listen to the reading of the Law and the Prophets, and hear discourses by teachers. Visitors were commonly given an opportunity to deliver the lecture or lesson. Jesus took advantage of these opportunities in his travels around Galilee to teach the worshipers in the synagogues.

4. Teaching on the mountain. No synagogue could hold the crowds drawn by Jesus during this phase of his ministry. According to the Gospel accounts, this was a period when Jesus was very popular.

Jesus, however, wanted the people to understand that he had not come to titillate them with sensational acts. He had come to lay upon them the demand of the gospel. The way to which he called them was a difficult and rugged way. He was not misled by his momentary popularity. The faith of the masses was superficial at best—the kind that has to be renewed daily by more and greater miracles. Jesus knew that few of them would be willing to walk the difficult, narrow way which he was about to set before them.

He went upon a mountain to teach them. The mountain is the place of revelation, where divine truths are given to men by God. Mountains are theologically significant in Matthew.

Jesus' disciples constituted the inner circle of the audience. They were the ones who had decided to follow him. He wanted to teach them what that decision implied.

Jesus sat down. This was the traditional posture of the teacher. In the synagogues one stood to read and sat to teach. What he taught is contained in the Sermon on the Mount, long understood by Christians to set forth the essence of what it means to follow Jesus. It has challenged and judged the disciples of the Lord in every generation.

II. The Beatitudes (Matt. 5:1-12)

In eight Beatitudes, Jesus sets forth the way of genuine ultimate happiness. The first four describe the attitudes necessary to receive God's promised blessing. The second group describes the characteristics of those who have made his blessing their goal.

1. Happiness, life's goal. Men have long thought of happiness as one of life's supreme goals. But what is happiness? Some think that they would really be happy if they could have a nice house with modern conveniences. They believe that the possession of things, like fur coats, automobiles, and swimming pools, will guarantee their happiness. For others, happiness is money in the bank. For still others it is success and fame. These are commonly held notions in spite of the fact that we also recognize that there is a lot of misery and unhappiness in palatial homes.

In the Beatitudes Jesus also talks about happiness. "Blessed" may be translated "how happy." But he talks about happiness in startling, paradoxical ways. True happiness is the possession, not of the rich but of the poor, not of those who laugh but of those who mourn.

He talked about happiness in this way because of his deep

convictions about God. He believed that genuine happiness can only be given by God. He also believed that the present circumstances of life are temporary and that people who sought life's ultimate meaning in them would be deluded. He believed that God would ultimately reward the faith of believers who spurned this world's alluring prizes for the promise of his blessings. These convictions are the foundations of the Beatitudes.

2. *The conditions for ultimate happiness.* Many readers of the Sermon on the Mount have a wrong approach to it. They say that it does not speak of grace but of law. They understand that it promises God's blessings to those who merit them by the quality of their performance. Salvation, they say, is presented as a reward for deeds rather than as a gift of love.

But they are wrong. The first four Beatitudes are the foundation for the total Sermon. They do not describe self-righteous achievers. Not at all. They talk about people who are conscious of their deep need and who rely solely on God to meet their need. The Sermon as a whole emphasizes the demand of the gospel, nevertheless, it begins with Beatitudes that set forth the meaning of grace—God's blessings are bestowed as unmerited favor upon his people.

They are given to the "poor in spirit." Luke omits "in spirit" (Luke 6:20), but Matthew has surely given the correct understanding of the Lukan Beatitude.

Poverty is not to be equated with happiness. As we all know, it can be a wretched, miserable, degrading circumstance. We should not use Jesus' statement as a justification for doing nothing about the gross economic inequities of society.

The poor mentioned in the Beatitude are people who recognize their own spiritual poverty and bankruptcy. They know that wealth is not the source of life's meaning and happiness. So they reject the false security of wealth and choose to depend on God and to serve him.

They may also be poor in material things. In fact, many times

God's people have had to choose between economic success and their faithfulness to him. Their loyalty to God may bring about their economic ruin, but they accept the consequence gladly.

Still others choose to give their lives in the service of God and his gospel and spurn the pursuit of wealth. So the poor in spirit may also be poor in worldly goods. But the important point is that they recognize the depth of their spiritual need.

"How happy are those who mourn." This is certainly a contra diction of popular ideas. When we see someone laughing, we commonly say, "He is really happy." But Jesus said, "Not so." There is a sadness that is a prerequisite to happiness. The person who recognizes his spiritual need is sad. He is also sad as he becomes sensitive to the evil and injustice in the world. His happiness results from his conviction that the way things are is not the way they will always be. True Christian joy, therefore, may be experienced even while one weeps because of a broken heart.

Happy people are "meek." This is a word that has been much misunderstood. It conjures up the picture of the weak, little person who is a doormat for everybody to walk on. But this is not the biblical meaning of meek. Moses was meek. So was Jesus. But neither one of them was a weak person with a poor self-image.

Meekness describes the believer's relationship to God. He does not have a low image of himself as a man. But he recognizes that he is only a man. He sees clearly his limitations and his weaknesses. In the light of this, he places his dependence entirely upon God, not in abdication of his manhood but as a fulfillment of it.

Happy people "hunger and thirst for righteousness." Righteousness may mean personal goodness. Or the Beatitude can refer to the believer's desire to see God's right prevail over the injustice and evil of the world. But more than likely the word means vindication. It is often used in the Old Testament as the equivalent of salvation (Isa. 51:5; Ps. 71:15). The believer, then, longs for the day when God will vindicate his faith by accepting him.

3. The gifts which produce happiness.   All the promises in the Beatitudes are in the passive voice. This is one of the reverential devices to avoid the mention of God's name. It is God who will give the promised blessings.

"The kingdom of heaven" is one of these gifts. Heaven is another circumlocution characteristic of Matthew used instead of God. The kingdom of heaven (of God) is the rule of God. To possess this rule means that the believer will share in all the benefits of God's reign.

For those who mourn there is the promise of ultimate comfort. The circumstances that produce mourning will be eliminated. We are reminded of the words of the Seer: "He will wipe away every tear from their eye" (Rev. 21:4).

God's people "will inherit the earth." "Earth" perhaps should be translated "land." The background of this promise is the Old Testament experience of Israel. They had been given the Promised Land as their inheritance. The new people of God also may look forward to receiving an inheritance in the promised land of the future.

Moreover, "they shall be satisfied." They have a longing, a sense of unfulfillment now. Nothing in this life or this world can satisfy it. They are the children of God, but they are buffeted by the winds of circumstance; they suffer from hostility and persecution. But God will vindicate them. He will one day show clearly who they really are and to whom they really belong.

4. The characteristics of God's people.   Jesus gives four characteristics of God's people in the last four Beatitudes.

They are "merciful," that is, forgiving, helping, encouraging. Sensitive to human need, they are quick to respond to it—not because the objects of their mercy are good or deserving but because sensitivity to human need expresses their own character as loving, compassionate people. Such merciful ones—forgiving, helping, encouraging ones—may face the future with confidence that God will respond to them in the same way.

Genuine disciples are "pure in heart." The heart is the center of man as a volitional, intellectual being. In ancient thought the seat of the emotions was not the heart but the viscera or intestines. In modern English, heart has more to do with emotions than will and intellect. Therefore, it often obscures the meaning of the text. The pure in heart are people who serve God with unmixed, unadulterated motives and devotion. Naturally, evil and immorality are a contradiction of this commitment.

People who serve God in single-minded devotion have the assurance that they "shall see him." The great longing of their life will be satisfied in the glorious vision of God.

God's people are peacemakers. They are actively involved in bringing about reconciliation and in building bridges of understanding.

Note that Jesus did not say "Blessed are the neutral." When tension and strife arise, most of us feel proud of ourselves if we stay neutral and do not take sides. But neutrality is not a Christian position. The Christian role is to work actively in order to bring hostile parties together and produce fellowship.

Peacemakers shall be called "sons of God." "Son of" is a commonly used expression which means "to partake of the nature of." To be a son of God, therefore, is to share in the nature and character of God.

God's primary purpose in the world is reconciliation. He is active in Christ to overcome the alienation between man and himself and to bring divided, hostile humanity together in a fellowship of love.

People who are working to engender hate and hostility are "sons of the devil." He works to produce hostility, prejudice, tensions, and divisions. The people who belong to God are found in the other camp.

God's people are "persecuted for righteousness' sake." Their commitment to justice, goodness, and compassion brings them into inevitable conflict with the unjust order of pagan society. We are not as aware of this in our society as we ought to be. In other times and in other places it has been perfectly clear that being a believer in Jesus involved suffering for your faith. When a public confession of faith in him brings an immediate reaction from society, such as the loss of a job, imprisonment, or the opposition of family, one does not make that confession lightly.

But in our society being a professed Christian is perfectly acceptable. No one is fired for being a member of our churches. No circles in society are automatically closed to him.

To be a genuine follower of Jesus, however, is not easy in any society. To champion the cause of justice, the rights of the poor and oppressed, or genuine Christian ethics always brings some form of persecution. Prophets are universally persecuted, for they challenge the evil in society in the name of one who loves justice and mercy.

But no matter how furious the opposition of the power structure, believers can take heart in the assurance that they will possess the kingdom. God is the genuine sovereign over their lives and over the world. They know that they can look forward to sharing in the benefits of his rule.

Their reward will be great in heaven (Matt. 5:11). The whole question of rewards is a difficult one in the Christian context. Is it a Christian motive to do without things now so that we can get more after awhile? Anyone will be willing to live in a cottage for a few years if he is assured that he can live in a mansion forever.

But we must remember that a reward in order to be a reward must have some value to the person to whom it is promised. If a person finds meaning in a life of love and service, why will the prospect of being exalted over others be attractive to him? Whatever the reward awaiting God's people in the future, it will be the kind of life that people who are merciful, peacemaking,

and who long above all else to serve God and see him will find
rich and meaningful.

III. Dangers to Discipleship (Matt. 5:13-16)

Disciples are salt and light. However, they face two
dangers. They may lose those characteristics which make
them salt, or they may fail to shine where light is needed.

1. The disciples as salt. We can hardly appreciate the strength
of the metaphor for Jesus' readers. Of course, we know that salt
gives flavor to foods, and we would hardly want to do without
it. But in the ancient world meats, for example, were preserved
by salting them or drying them. Salt, therefore, was one of the
precious commodities of antiquity.

In order to give taste to food or to preserve it, salt had to
retain its saltlike characteristics. Now, it is true that salt is always
salt. But the salt used by people in Palestine was often an adulter-
ated variety. It came from the area of the Dead Sea and had
gypsum mixed in it. Gypsum looked like salt but did not have
its characteristics. It could neither preserve nor give taste to food.

When Jesus said that his disciples were salt of the earth, he
was implying something about the earth and his followers. The
earth, that is, human society, was subject to corruption and decay.
The disciples were to function among men as elements that would
halt the evil process of corruption.

But disciples could lose those qualities which enabled them
to stay the forces of corruption. What were those characteristics?
We probably could name many. In the context we may say that
they are the characteristics mentioned in the beatitudes—mercy,
reconciliation, righteousness. These are the forces that stay the
power of hatred, prejudice, and evil in society. Without these
characteristics, disciples cannot fulfill their role in the world.

2. Disciples as light. Unlike salt, light could not cease to be
light. But the effect of light could be negated by putting it under
a bushel. If you light a lamp and hide it under a container, the

room will be just as dark as if there were no light in it.

Conversely light put in a prominent place can be seen from great distance. Jesus illustrated this by reference to a city located on a hill. We remember that most ancient cities were built on prominent places for defense purposes.

Disciples are light. As light they cannot help but shine. However, their light may be so hidden that it does not shine in the dark places of the world. Men who are in darkness will not see the light.

Jesus may have had the Essene community of Qumran in mind. These people claimed to be the righteous, pure, genuine followers of God. They had removed themselves from the evil of Jewish society and built a monastic community northwest of the Dead Sea.

Jesus did not want his followers to follow that example. Unfortunately in the course of Christian history many of them have failed to follow his teachings. There is always the tendency for Christians to withdraw from corrupt society in an effort to escape its evil influence and to maintain their purity.

Jesus urged his disciples, "Let your light shine *before men.*" He did not command them to let their light shine (as a popular chorus interprets it). We have seen that light, if it is light, cannot do anything but shine. Jesus was concerned, rather, about the place where it would shine. He wanted his followers to be in the midst of the world, dispelling the darkness of greed, hostility, and immorality.

The purpose, naturally, is not to attract attention to one's self but to bring men to the source of their life, that is, to God himself. The Christian will fulfill his role as light if he helps men to recognize God as God and to praise him for his love, goodness, and mercy which produce the light that shines in the lives of believers.

4.
The Greater Righteousness
5:17-48

I. Jesus and the Law (Matt. 5:17-20)

Jesus declares that he is the fulfiller and not the abolisher of the law. His way is not to be thought of as an easy one. To the contrary, it is much more demanding than the way of the law followed by Jewish religious leaders.

1. A misunderstanding of the gospel. The gospel is both grace and demand. We have noted that the Sermon on the Mount begins with an emphasis on grace. Only people who recognize the depth of their need and depend solely upon God have the assurance of ultimate happiness. Conversely, self-righteous persons who depend upon their own moral achievements do not have a saving relationship with God.

But the gospel of grace is always subject to misunderstanding. We know that when Paul preached about grace, many people misunderstood him (see Rom. 6:1 ff.). They interpreted him to mean that the gospel absolves men from moral responsibility. They felt that since they were saved by grace, they did not have to be concerned by morals and ethics. Some of them went so far as to teach that men did God a favor by sinning. The more they sinned, the more grace was needed. According to this perverted notion, they magnified the gospel of grace by sinning. They taught that Jesus had abolished the law of the Old Testament and that it was no longer of any significance for believers. We call these people libertines.

This section of the Sermon warns against that kind of attitude.

The gospel is closely related to the law. Jesus did not want people to get the idea that he had come to abolish the law. His purpose was to fulfill it.

2. *Jesus the fulfiller of the law.* As we have said, the libertine position that the law is no longer important or worthy of notice is wrong. But we are faced with the question: "What does it mean to say that Jesus fulfilled the law?"

It certainly does not mean what some modern Christian legalists take it to mean. They say that the law is just as binding as it ever was. Christians are responsible for observing all the commandments of the Old Testament in every detail. According to them, the gospel gives believers the power to live by the law, a power which Jews lacked.

This is obviously a false position. Jesus himself did away with certain of the commandments and provisions of the Old Testament (see Matt. 5:31-36). So the fulfillment of the law involved doing away with certain provisions of it. No doubt Jesus could have multiplied these examples.

Jesus fulfilled the law in the sense that what he did and taught was in keeping with the purpose of God in giving the law. God's purpose, as revealed in the Bible, is to create a people who will love and serve him and one another. This purpose was behind God's dealing with Israel, including his giving of the law, and it was brought to fruition in the life of Jesus the Messiah. In this way the law, seen in its totality, is fulfilled.

What is the proper Christian approach to the law? It is neither to treat it with disdain by breaking it and teaching others to break it, nor to become its slave by applying it legalistically. Rather, we should try to relate the law to what God has done in Christ in order to find its true meaning and be guided by it. In so doing, we shall be accepting the claim of Jesus that he was the fulfiller of the law.

3. *The demand of the gospel.* Jesus did not come to teach men to break the law. Rather, he came to lead them into a higher righteousness than that reached by those who lived by the law.

The problem with the scribes and Pharisees was not that they did too much but rather that they did too little. Scribes were the experts in the law. They had developed a massive oral tradition to tell men how to order every detail of their lives by the law. Pharisees were people who attempted to live by that tradition. They were extremely moral and religious people.

But Jesus said that their righteousness was not good enough. The righteousness of his followers was not to be less than that of the people who lived by the law as they understood it. Rather, it was to go far beyond it. Beginning with verse 21, Jesus gives six illustrations of the righteousness which exceeds that of the Jewish religious leaders.

II. The Righteousness of the Gospel (Matt. 5:21-48)

Jesus uses six Commandments from the Old Testament to show how the righteousness of his disciples must go far beyond that practiced by people who lived by those commandments.

1. Murder. The law against murder is one of the Ten Commandments. The man who committed murder was subject to the judgment or sentence of death. According to the prevalent view in Jesus' time, a person could think of himself as a keeper of that law if he did not actually take another man's life.

But Jesus' command goes beyond the legalistic observance of that law to the attitudes which generate murder. Jesus demanded more than a mere outward compliance with the law. He demanded an inner righteousness and purity which can be judged by no court.

So a man who is angry with his brother is also a murderer. Some later manuscripts insert "without cause" into verse 22, but it does not belong to the original teaching of Jesus. The man who is angry with his brother is worthy of the same punishment as an actual murderer. Indeed, there is no difference in the attitude and spirit of the two. As we know from the ample illustrations of contemporary life, the individual who is the victim of boiling fires of rage is a potential murderer.

It should be said that there is a righteous anger about which the Bible speaks in other places that does not fall into this category. Furthermore, all of us get angry at times with people we love dearly—our wives, our children, and our friends.

One of the major human problems is that we do not acknowledge, express appropriately, and deal with this kind of anger. And suppressed, unresolved anger can develop into the kind of murderous rage that Jesus is talking about.

Another attitude that can lead to murder is contempt for the other. Such contempt is expressed in insulting, deprecating remarks like "you fool." The annihilation of millions of Jews in Germany was made possible by a common attitude of contempt toward them. If men regard any individual as less than human in the fullest sense, a major restraint on murder is removed.

There are people who would not dare call another person a fool, because Jesus expressly forbad it. But if Jesus were among us, he may have forbidden the use of words like Chink, honky, nigger, pig, and gook.

Man's relationship to God is inextricably bound up with his relationship to his brother. A barrier between him and his brother is at the same time a barrier between him and God.

Genuine worship is possible only when estranged brothers are reconciled. The worshiper who comes to the altar when his fellowship with his brother is broken needs to repair that relationship before his sacrifice to God will be accepted.

The passage ends with an illustration which is a warning. A man who is being brought into court because he owes something to another will try to avert a sentence by making arrangements to pay the debt. Debtors were harshly treated in those days, as the illustration shows.

We, too, are going toward judgment. It is far better to effect reconciliation with our offended brother than to come before God with this kind of debt on our record.

2. *Adultery.* The law against adultery was rather narrowly defined among the Jews. Adultery was specifically sexual relations with another man's wife. Men who had not had sexual relations with the wife of another congratulated themselves on being righteous with regard to this commandment.

But Jesus once again lifts morality to a higher level. Adultery is not only the overt act as defined by the religious experts. An adulterer is a man who lusts after any woman.

The basic problem here is the same as the one in murder. It is essentially a contempt for the other person that makes it possible to use her (or him) for one's own personal selfish satisfaction. It is a violation of the law of love which demands that we put the other's welfare and happiness above our own.

We need to understand that the problem is not our sexuality nor our sexual feelings. Too many Christians have felt that sexual feelings themselves are wrong and have borne a tremendous burden of guilt because they had the kind of feelings and urges which God created us to have.

The problem is in our basic attitude toward people. Lust causes us to treat persons as objects, as things. Love demands that we honor their personhood as sacred, not to be desecrated or cheapened in order to satisfy our sexual urges.

Jesus recommends that people who are inclined to use others to fulfill their sexual needs deal with the problem in a radical way. His illustrations, naturally, must be understood as metaphors. A man with one eye or one hand can still be guilty of using another person sexually.

There is a man (his name is legion) who has had one illicit affair after another. I believe that he has been reaching out for love because of his lack of it in early childhood. But he has been reaching out in destructive ways—destructive to himself, his family, and the women he has used. What he needed to do long ago was to face up to his problem and do whatever was necessary to come to grips with it. He has not submitted to the kind of radical surgery necessary to excise his problem and, as a result, has lived a demeaning, tortured existence.

3. *Divorce.* The law attempted to regulate marriage relations in order to give some minimal protection to women. It required, therefore, that a man give his wife a certificate of divorce, which at least declared that she no longer belonged to him. This to some extent clarified her position in society.

The rabbinic scholars were divided about the interpretation of Deuteronomy 24:1, that is, about the proper grounds for divorce. The school of Hillel contended that a man could divorce his wife on almost any ground. The conservative school of Shammai held that adultery alone was the ground of divorce. The teaching of Jesus as given in Matthew 5:32 is in line with this point of view. Many scholars, however, believe that the "except clause" was introduced later in the teaching of Jesus. They do not think that an exception is in accord with the radical teaching of Jesus elsewhere in the sermon. Also, the exception is not included in a parallel passage in Mark (Mark 10:11-12).

Jesus taught that marriage was intended by God to be a lifetime relationship and that the divorce provision of the law was a temporary arrangement (see Matt. 19:8), a concession, as it were, to man's sinfulness.

An obvious problem arises for us in the teaching of Jesus. He says that the man who divorces his wife "makes her an adulteress." From what we know about Jesus, however, we cannot believe that this was God's judgment on an innocent woman who happened to be the victim of a callous, unfeeling husband. Rather, he was talking about her position in society. Although she had been divorced for some petty reason, her position in society would be the same as that of a woman who had been divorced for adultery. Moreover, any marriage that she contracted would be stigmatized by her divorce.

The teachings of Jesus was uttered in a male-dominated society where women had few rights. Today, however, women can also initiate divorce action and so bear much more responsibility in the breakdown of marriage than they did in the ancient world.

Another serious question is raised at this point. God's will for marriage is that the couple will maintain their relationship until parted by death. But what about people who cannot live up to that ideal?

Too often we have misunderstood the Sermon on the Mount and have taken it as a new law by which we judge if people are good or bad. This is especially true with reference to this issue. We do not, for example, regard people who fail to live up to God's ideal of love in Matthew 5:44 in the same way that we do those who fail to live up to his ideal for marriage in Matthew 5:31-32. There is really no biblical or theological reason for this difference.

This attitude leads to some strange inconsistencies. I heard an evangelist who told about how immoral he was before he was saved. Everybody thought his testimony was wonderful. But if he had made the mistake of marrying one of the women with whom he had sexual relations, probably he would not have been invited to preach in that church. In this connection, we might ask, how many churches could have deacons and preachers if we were able to eliminate all adulterers as defined by Jesus in Matthew 5:28?

Does the gospel have anything to say to people who experience failure in living up to the Christian ideal? Is the only thing that we can say: "You should have been wiser, more careful, or more persevering?"

The word of the gospel to people who fail is the word of grace. There is no failure for which forgiveness is not available. The gospel declares that a person can begin all over again at any moment, no matter what his failure in the past.

4. Oaths. According to the Old Testament, people were permitted to take oaths in the name of God. But they were commanded to fulfill their oaths, that is, not to commit perjury.

Jewish people realized how serious it was to swear to do something in the name of God. They might not be able to keep their word and so would be guilty of breaking the law. So the custom had arisen to swear by less serious things, that is, heaven, the earth, and so forth.

But Jesus forbids oath-taking of any kind. What he demanded was basic integrity. A man's word should be his bond. His simple statement or promise should be just as binding as any oath he might take. An unqualified yes or no should be sufficient without any oaths to support them.

Once again certain groups have made a new legalism out of the Sermon. They refuse to take an oath in a court of law. But this is to miss the point altogether. Jesus did not teach that oath-taking was wrong in itself. What he did teach was that we should be so honest and responsible that we would not need to take an oath to ensure that we would keep our word.

5. Retaliation. The law's requirement of an "eye for an eye" represented a decided advance in ancient justice. In practice, oftentimes people were excessively punished for minor offences. There is a commendable equity, therefore, in the Old Testament concept. We must also remember that the criminal code was also a part of the religious law, since there was no distinction between church and state.

But Jesus declares that this precept is inadequate for his followers. Once again in fulfilling the law, or going beyond it to a higher level in order to achieve God's purpose in giving it, Jesus sets aside a provision in the law itself.

The disciple of Jesus does not respond to injury in terms defined by the law of the Old Testament. He does not demand in the name of justice that his offender be caused to suffer an equal amount. Jesus, however, does not ask his follower to be a passive recipient of injury. No! Rather, he is to respond in a totally unexpected, positive way. When struck on one cheek, he is to turn the other.

The blow on the face is the insulting blow, designed to humiliate or to provoke hostile reaction. But it does not accomplish this end with reference to the true disciple of Jesus. Most of us have not been slapped on the cheek recently. But many have been offended or humiliated in other ways. The question is, do we strike back? Do we repay evil with evil? Or do we turn the other cheek by doing a positive good for the person who has offended us?

Jesus gave two further illustrations of the kind of attitude demanded of his followers. One is drawn from the judicial process. A debtor could be sued and forced to turn over his tunic, the commonly-worn inner garment, to his creditor. But the cloak, the outer garment, was considered essential to life. It served as a bed-covering by night and a garment by day. It could not be taken from a person in a law suit. But Jesus instructed his hearers to surrender the cloak also.

What does this mean? It means that Christians are to go further in their relations with others than the law demands. Perhaps a modern illustration of this would be the believer who is forced into bankruptcy by untoward business conditions. According to law, he does not have to pay that part of his debt which his assets do not cover. But he works the rest of his life to pay the debt in order to live up to his own standards as a Christian.

In the time of Jesus, it must have been common for Roman soldiers to force Jews to carry their packs. You can imagine the hostility and hatred which flamed up in the heart of a man forced into this subservient role. How glad he was to reach the end of the required mile! How quickly he threw down the hated burden! But Jesus instructed his followers to act in a totally different way. When forced to go one mile, they were to go another voluntarily. Great Christians through the ages have found tremendous freedom in this sort of response to slavery. Their masters can compel them to perform certain tasks, but there is something which they cannot compel. It is the service of love. This is something the Christian can give out of the wealth of his inner resources.

The spirit of revenge is forbidden to the disciple. Its opposite, the spirit of open-handed generosity, is to determine his relation to others. There is much to be said about the matter of giving and lending which is not contained in Jesus' single statement here. Whether we give to someone should be determined by the principle of love, that is, what is best for him. But, if we do not give what is asked of us, it should not be because of a lack of generosity on our part. Jesus commands his followers to act in a generous, free spirit.

6. Love your enemies. The law commands love for the neighbor (Lev. 19:18). It contains no injunction to hate the enemy. But the question is, who is my neighbor? Who are the people I must love? If I can define them, then I have defined the limit of my responsibility to this law, for it does not tell me to love those who are not my neighbors. I may interpret the law, therefore, as allowing me to hate them.

In the Bible the antithesis of love-hate usually defines the whole range of possible relations to people. Anything less than love is hate. Negligence and indifference fall into the category of hate.

Jewish people usually identified their neighbors as fellow members of the covenant community. They were Israelites and proselytes. Samaritans and foreigners were not neighbors. If Jews hated Samaritans, therefore, they did not believe that this was a violation of the law. In fact, by implication it was permissible and even demanded by the law of love as they interpreted it.

But Jesus rejected the common interpretation of the law. His disciples were to love not only their fellow Jews but also Samaritans and foreigners. They were even to love the despised Roman oppressors. They were to pray for people who persecuted them.

The character of the disciple was to be determined by the

character of God. His love, expressed in the beneficent providence of nature, was extended to all men—even to the evil and the unjust. God loved men who despised him, disregarded his commandments, and worshiped false gods.

This love of God, designated by the Greek word *agape* in the New Testament, does not arise in response to the character or the attitude of its recipient. God's love arises out of and is determined by his own nature. It expresses the central aspect of his character. He loves because it is his nature to love. His love cannot be deterred or quenched by anything outside it.

How can the disciple show that he is the grateful recipient of God's love? It cannot be done in the normal, reciprocal patterns of human relationships. That is, we cannot demonstrate *agape* by loving only people who are good and kind to us. The tax collectors, considered by Jews to be among the worst of sinners, responded to love with love. Even pagans recognized and esteemed the people of their own inner circle. They did not ignore their friends but greeted them warmly when they encountered them.

It is no evidence of the grace of God, therefore, to love people who love us. It is only in loving people who injure us, talk about us, or in some other way offend us that we can demonstrate that we know the love of God.

Jesus concludes his statement about love for the enemy with the injunction: "You, therefore, must be perfect, as your heavenly Father is perfect." The word perfect in this context means mature. God's perfection or maturity is determined solely by who he is, not by who they are.

As long as we react to men in terms of their actions and attitudes toward us, we are immature. We are perfect or mature when our actions are determined by our character as the children of God. We love men, not because they deserve to be loved, but because it is in keeping with our own nature as believers.

5.
Treasures in Heaven

6:1-34

I. The Peril of Being Religious (Matt. 6:1-18)

Jesus warns his disciples against practicing religious acts in order to impress others with their piety. He illustrates his warning with three practices which were very important in Jewish religious life—almsgiving, praying, and fasting.

1. The warning. In an earlier passage (Matt. 5:16), Jesus instructed his disciples to let their light shine before men. Here he tells them not to practice their piety before men. What are we to make of this?

We should understand, first of all that the practices in the two passages are different. In the previous passage, it is the disciple's light that is to shine before men. Light must be understood as the qualities of mercy, peacemaking, purity, and justice whose source is God. In this passage, the subject of discussion is piety. The underlying Greek word is actually righteousness (as in the King James Version). But from the context we know that it is righteousness understood in terms of pious or religious activities.

In each case, also, the motivation is different, and that is the important matter. On the one hand, the disciples are to live and act in order to cause men to glorify God. On the other hand, they are commanded not to engage in religious practices to bring praise upon themselves.

The basic problem in this passage is not the nature of the acts themselves. There is nothing intrinsically wrong with charity, prayer, or fasting. All may be commendable Christian activities.

Jesus condemns none of them. He does warn against using them to make other people think that one is religiously superior.

If Jesus were speaking in our day he probably would use different illustrations. He might say: "Don't go to church to be seen of men." Or, he might warn against using things like reading the Bible in order to make people think that we are spiritual. The passage calls our attention to a real problem. Any religious practice may be turned into an evil if it is done for the wrong reason. When we engage in religious practices in order to demonstrate our spiritual superiority to other people, we pervert them, and they become evil. When our religious practices make us feel that we need God's grace less than people who neglect them, they also become evil.

2. The practices. Evidently much in common religious practices of his day led Jesus to conclude that they arose out of a desire for attention and praise. Many people gave money to the poor, not because of their sensitivity to human need, nor as a genuine service of gratitude to God for their own blessings, but to enhance their own reputation and to receive the plaudits of the crowd. Because this was their motive, they had to make sure that people saw them when they gave. They "sounded a trumpet" to call attention to their deed.

We are not sure if they literally blew a trumpet or not. It is possible that a trumpet was sounded when an especially large gift was made in the synagogue on occasions of public fund-raising for the needy. However, "sound the trumpet" is probably figurative, denoting any method used to call attention to one's gift.

Evidently it was a common practice for religious people to pray in public so that people would know that they were pious. When they were fasting, they smeared ashes on their faces and left their hair and beard untended. Anyone who saw them could tell at a glance that they were fasting.

Fasting is mentioned frequently in the Old Testament, especially in connection with national peril or crisis. However, the only fast commanded by the law was the annual fast associated with the Day of Atonement. But the Pharisees had made fasting a regular religious practice, engaging in it on Mondays and Thursdays. It had become one of the badges of the pious man.

Jesus did not abolish any of these practices. He assumed that his followers would engage in all of them. But he advised them to practice their religious acts in a way so as not to call public attention to them.

These statements by Jesus have often been wrongly interpreted. Some people have used them to justify their own failure to give money as responsible members of the Christian community. There is no reason why a group of Christians cannot come together, determine what the financial obligations of their church will be, and pledge their appropriate share in meeting that responsibility. Jesus himself is shown to have paid the Temple tax publicly.

There is also nothing wrong with public prayers in the congregation of worshipers. Jesus participated frequently in the worship of the synagogue which featured public prayers. Jesus, therefore, did not have corporate worship in view here.

3. The principle. If a person does something to gain attention and praise from others and his act does in fact cause people to think of him as religious, righteous, or spiritual, then he has achieved his goal. He can expect nothing beyond this. He has received the plaudits of men. His efforts are justly compensated. He has the reward for which he strives.

This idea is brought out by the phrase "they have their reward" (v. 2). The verb in the phrase was used to mark receipts. "They have their reward" could be translated "they have been paid in full." Jesus taught that people who engaged in ostentatious display of their piety need not, indeed, they should not, expect anything from God. When other people saw them and praised them for being righteous, they could consider themselves "paid in full."

But if the goal of life is to please God and to serve for his glory alone, then one must take another approach. God honors the deed that is done with no thought of selfish gain or glory. The truly Christian life is lived in the faith that the only account that is worth keeping is the one kept by God.

4. The Lord's Prayer.   In Matthew the Lord's Prayer is given in the context of the Sermon. It is found elsewhere and in slightly different terms in Luke (see Luke 11:2-4).

This prayer, sometimes called the Model Prayer, begins with the two basic presuppositions of Christian prayer. The first of these is the conviction that God is "Father." Matthew has the more liturgical "Our Father," whereas Luke has the simple "Father." The latter is Jesus' more characteristic address when speaking to God. It is the Semitic *Abba*, and was the term children used to address their fathers. No doubt it was often the very first word that the child learned to say. The English equivalent to *ab-ba* would be da-da. It is, therefore, an intimate word that expresses the relationship of a little child to his father. It is the name for that person in whom the child trusts completely to care for him and meet his needs.

Second, the supreme desire of the believer is for God to be honored and his will to be done. God is holy, and man cannot make him holier than he is. But men can fail to honor him as God. They show their disrespect for him in many ways. They ignore him, rebel against him, are profane and evil. In the Bible, "name" stands for the person. The prayer "hallowed be thy name," is a plea, therefore, that men everywhere acknowledge God as holy and that they live in reverent relation to him.

We go to God with our petitions and needs. And rightly so. But our desire is not for our will to be done but his. We do not want to be in charge. We want his kingdom to come. That is, we long for the victory of his rule over all the forces of evil.

The Lord's Prayer must be personal if it is to have any meaning at all. Too often when men pray "Thy kingdom come, thy will be done," they are thinking about their neighbor. We cannot pray sincerely "Thy kingdom come" unless we want God to rule our own lives. We cannot pray sincerely "Thy will be done" unless we genuinely want God's will to be done in us personally.

The Lord's Prayer also recognizes the believer's dependence on God's providence to supply the physical necessities of life. Bread stands for those things which are essential to our physical existence.

The average reader of the New Testament may be surprised to learn that "daily" represents the translation of a difficult word. Some of the church fathers took the position that Jesus was unconcerned about physical things. So they translated the word as "spiritual," "essential," and so forth. But they were doubtless mistaken.

The best understanding of "daily" is probably "that which is necessary for today." God gives us life one moment at a time. If we have enough to meet our basic human needs for today, then we should be able to face the future with the faith that God will provide our needs on any future days he may give us.

Jewish people thought of sin as a debt owed to God. Jesus used this metaphor in several of his parables—the unrighteous steward (Matt. 18:21-35), the two debtors (Luke 7:36-50), and the unprofitable servant (Luke 17:7-10). Our debts, therefore, are our sins against God. Our debtors are the people who have wronged us in some way.

Jesus linked God's forgiveness of us with our forgiveness of persons who offend us. But we should not understand our forgiveness of our debtors as being antecedent to and a necessary requirement of our receiving forgiveness from God. The English translation could give this idea. Rather, our action of forgiveness is simultaneous with our reception of forgiveness. The tenses in the Greek text point to this interpretation.

My professor, Frank Stagg, used to express it in this way: "The person who is unforgiving is unforgiven because he is unforgivable." That is, the capacity to receive forgiveness is at the same time the capacity to forgive. How can a person who perceives his tremendous need for God's grace be at the same time hard and unforgiving toward another who has a similar need?

"Lead us not into temptation." But we read elsewhere that God is not the source of temptation. How, then, are we to understand this petition?

First, the word translated "temptation" also means "trial" or "testing." God is not the author of temptation, but he does lead us to make commitments, take stands, and engage in activities that can result in testing or trials. For example, many faithful Christians have been tested by persecution. God is not the author of the evil hatred which produces persecution. He does not will persecution, but he does will that we remain steadfast in the face of persecution and trials.

Perhaps the best illustration of the meaning of this petition if found in connection with the Gethsemane experience of Jesus (Matt. 26:41). He instructed his disciples to ask God to deliver them from temptation. The reason is given: "The flesh is weak." That is, they were not strong enough for the terrible events that lay ahead. All that was left to them was to ask God not to lead them into water that was over their heads. The disciples slept instead of praying, and they failed when the hour of testing came. One wonders if the story might have been different had the disciples been sensitive to the situation and followed Jesus' advice.

No one of us knows the limits of his strength. The prayer "Lead us not into temptation" is a humble recognition that there are circumstances which would probably be beyond our strength. None of us knows his breaking point. We can only ask that God not lead us into situations in which we would be unfaithful to him. "Deliver us from evil" or, it may be, "the evil one" is simply a repetition of the same request.

The liturgical closing of the prayer, "for thine is the kingdom," and so forth, is not in modern versions. It is not supported by readings from the oldest and best manuscripts. It is an addition made by Christians as they used the prayer in public worship.

Of course it is a thoroughly Christian statement.

II. The Peril of Possessions (Matt. 6:19-24)

Jesus shows that the danger confronting a man who has material things is that he may fall into idolatry. By placing an idolatrous value on possessions, he takes a course which causes him to waste his life and which endangers his total self. He must choose between God and possessions.

1. The peril of idolatry. Jesus had a great deal to say about possessions. But his emphasis was different from the one we usually hear in our churches today. Church leaders generally urge people to give in order to support the institution, to undergird missionary work, and the like. In other words, the emphasis is on the results of giving, what can be done with wealth.

Jesus was not insensitive to human need and what could be done with money to alleviate that need (see Matt. 25:35). His major concern, however, was with people who had money. Most of his teaching on wealth relates to the people who possessed it and the danger it presented for them.

The major peril of wealth is that people tend to make it their god. The man who worships wealth is an idolater. It occupies in his life the place that God alone should occupy.

"Treasure" represents that which is of most value to a person. It is what he loves most and prizes most highly. Jesus points out the folly of making earthly things the goal of life. They are subject to the processes of deterioration and decay. Rust eats away at them. Moths consume them. They can always be taken away by another who wants them badly enough to steal. So earthly treasures are very poor gods. One can never be sure of them.

Rather, Jesus cautions men to "lay up treasures in heaven" that are not subject to decay or theft. You lay up treasures in heaven by serving God and making his will supreme. Deeds of love, mercy, and righteousness have lasting value.

Your heart will be where your treasure is. Heart in biblical thought is generally associated with will and intellect. It is often synonymous with mind. Jesus understood that people would focus their attention on, dedicate themselves to, and spend their energies in attaining that which was most valuable to them.

2. The effect of stinginess on life.   The "sound eye" is idiomatic for a generous spirit. The "evil eye" is an expression for a stingy spirit. Jesus was aware that generosity or stinginess pervaded the whole personality. If a person has a generous spirit, it will affect his whole being. A stingy spirit has the opposite effect. It spreads darkness in every area of life.

We fail to understand this important principle. You cannot compartmentalize, isolate, and confine evil once it has entered your life. If a person hates anybody for any reason, he is capable of hating others. If a person is stingy in one area of his life, he is apt to be stingy in all others. Or, as Jesus expressed it, "if your eye is not sound, your whole body will be full of darkness."

3. The ultimate choice.   Finally, Jesus lays down the guiding principle. You cannot serve, that is, be a slave to, two masters. It is impossible to give your ultimate loyalty to more than one person. Thus, you must make a choice. If money is of ultimate value to you, you cannot serve the true God.

There are many people who go to church regularly, sing songs, and recite Scripture passages but who are really idolaters. They are idolaters because money is more important to them than anything else, including God.

III. The Problem of Anxiety (Matt. 6:25-34)

Jesus asks his disciples not to be anxious about their future physical needs. He points out that anxiety is the opposite of trust in God and that it is useless.

1. The cause of anxiety.   There is an inevitable consequence of the worship of wealth. The man who does so will be afflicted with anxiety. He has made money the basis of his security. But he always knows that his god may fail him some time in the future. So he has to live with the anxiety produced by the possibility of this failure.

Jesus advises men "not to be anxious" about material things. He does not rule out thoughtful, creative planning for the present and a possible future. He certainly did not intend that men be lazy, shiftless, or nonproductive. Anxiety is fruitless, futile, self-defeating worry about a future that God has not given us yet and may never give us. Anxiety is the opposite of faith. It causes a person to bear the burden of the future—and a human being is not equipped to bear this load. Faith, on the other hand, trusts God with the future. This liberates the individual so he can bring his strength, talents, and creative energy to bear on solving today's problems and meeting today's challenges and needs.

Too many people are not able to enjoy the meal that they have today for fear that they may not have one out there in the future. Too many people are unable to live today because they are eaten up with anxieties about tomorrow.

2. Trust in God as the cure for anxiety. Jesus emphasized an important truth as he began to deal with this problem. We may be able to store up some food for the future and have some clothes in mothballs for next winter. But we cannot guarantee that there will be a body to be clothed or a mouth to eat the food next winter. Life is a gift from God. We have to trust him for it. And he gives it one day at a time. He who gives us life also is able to make provisions to meet life's necessities.

Anxiety is faithless. The anxious person can learn a lesson from nature. God has made provision in his world for the lowest of his creatures. God provides for birds, which are totally free from anxieties experienced by man. The lilies which are part of God's creation, completely dependent upon him, lacking in creativity to provide for their own needs, are more beautiful than any splendor that could be bought by Solomon's vast wealth. Can we not believe that a loving father will provide for man who is the highest of all his creatures?

Numerous questions may be raised in this connection. There are starving people in the world. That is an undeniable fact. But is the basic problem located in a lack of provision by God in nature for his creatures? Or does the major difficulty lie in human greed and selfishness? There is enough food to provide for basic human needs if we who have more than our share were unselfish enough to solve the problem. And if we used our God-given intelligence to deal with the problems of population and food distribution.

Anxiety is useless. Anxiety may be produced by many causes. But Jesus is dealing here with anxiety that is produced by worry over one's own contined physical existence. He says something which we all know in our hearts. Anxiety does not add "one cubit to the span of life."

A cubit was the distance from the elbow to the tip of the middle finger, eighteen inches, more or less. The word translated "span of life" can also mean "statue" and is so translated in the KJV. This, however, would be an enormous amount to add to one's height. It is better to translate "span of life" with the RSV. This, after all, is the subject of Jesus' remarks. And a cubit added to the length of life would signify only a blink of the eye.

No, anxiety cannot increase one's physical existence. Ironically, it does take away from life expectancy. The people who worry most about future financial security are apt to have less time to enjoy the things they do have.

Anxiety is pagan. Jesus remarked that Gentiles, that is, pagans, are driven by a desire to acquire worldly possessions. And well they might be. Their gods were capricious and arbitrary. Gentiles did not believe that their gods were really concerned about them. Indeed, those gods could be against them, making their situation worse.

But Christians believe that God is a Father. He is a Father who loves his children, knows their needs, and wants to help. This means that they are not alone in a hostile universe.

3. *Putting first things first.* Jesus instructs his disciples, therefore, to seek God's kingdom first. They do not have to make the acquisition of things their primary concern. Faith in God frees them from this. They can make God's rule the most important thing in their life. When God is made King of one's life, everything takes on its proper perspective. Working is not wrong. Earning a living is not wrong. Social security is not wrong. Indeed, to provide for one's needs and make plans for a possible old age can be genuine acts of love. We do not want to be a burden to someone else. The problem is one of emphasis. God and not wealth is to be of first importance in our lives.

Jesus' concluding remark (v. 34) is one that can be paraphrased by a common saying: "Don't cross your bridges before you get to them."

Most of us have problems enough and challenges enough in the present to occupy all our resources. We can rest assured that any tomorrow will have its own needs and difficulties to face. We can face our problems today in the conviction that God will be with us tomorrow, whatever happens, just as he is with us today.

6.
The Narrow Gate

7:1-29

I. On Judging (Matt. 7:1-6)

Jesus warns against judging others. He instructs his disciple to remove the log from his own eye before taking the speck out of his brother's. In any case, he cautions his followers against giving their pearls of insight to people who cannot appreciate them.

1. The sin of judging. Judging is essentially idolatrous. It is an attempt by man to seize a prerogative which belongs to God and to God alone.

A human being is in no position to judge another because of two serious limitations. In the first place, he does not have all the facts. He is limited to the outward and visible aspects of character. Usually he is not even aware of all these more or less objective data. He surely cannot know the heart. He cannot see motives; he cannot assess causes of actions properly.

In the second place, no person is good enough to judge another. We are all sinners and all stand in the same relationship to God's demands.

Most of us would agree that chicken-stealing is not as serious as murder. But we do not, for this reason, make the thief the judge of the murderer.

But that is exactly the position we assume when we presume to judge others. We conclude that our acts are not as bad as the acts of our neighbor, which gives us the prerogative of judging him, whatever may be his faults.

There are two ways of perceiving God. One of them is to perceive him only as a lawgiver who demands that men live up to his commandments. The person who fails to fulfill his requirements is unrighteous and, therefore, worthy of condemnation.

Another way to perceive God is in terms of the central truth of the gospel. God is gracious. He accepts and forgives men who do not measure up to the divine imperatives.

However we perceive God, we should realize that we cannot have it both ways. It is inconsistent to think of God as a lawgiver who rejects and condemns our sinful brother but at the same time accepts and forgives us. If our brother stands under God's judgment, we stand at his side under the same judgment. If God rejects our brother because of his sins, he will reject us because of our sins. The judgment by which we judge others also condemns us.

On the other hand, if God accepts us and is merciful to us in spite of our sins, he will relate to our brother in the same way. The point of Jesus' teaching is this: We have not understood our own need for mercy if we are unmerciful in our attitude toward others.

2. Responsibility for the brother. The refusal to judge does not mean that one is morally insensitive or blind. Our brother is indeed a sinner who needs help. In the words of Jesus, he does have a "speck in his eye." And we are responsible for helping him in his weakness.

But we cannot help the erring brother if our attitude is arrogant and self-righteous. Our sin must always be greater to us than the sin of the brother. Sadly the reverse is generally the case. We see our sin as the speck or the splinter and the sin of our brother as the log. So long as we persist in this point of view we cannot help him with his problems. We must reverse the ratio. Our sin in comparison to the sin of the brother is in the ratio of log to splinter. When we recognize the extent of our faults and the depth of our own need for grace, we shall be in the position to help others in their moral and spiritual struggles.

God never intended that we struggle with our temptations and sins alone. We need the help, insight, and support of our brothers. We need grace and acceptance, but we cannot learn of grace from judgmental people who have not experienced it. When we sin, we need the help of people who know God as a forgiving God in their own lives.

3. *Pearls before swine.* The Gospels give us many isolated statements of Jesus without the broader context needed for a confident interpretation. Such is the case with his prohibition against giving holy things to dogs or throwing pearls before swine.

The central truth is clear. The disciple of Jesus must exercise judgment and discretion in his communication of the truths of the gospel. Many people are as insensitive to the worth of those truths as pigs are to the value of pearls. There are occasions when it is better to remain silent than to speak. If we are insensitive to the situation or to the reactions and attitudes of other people, we may make matters worse by speaking. Instead of helping them, we may make them worse, even inciting them to violence.

If we do not speak, it should not be for the lack of courage. It should rather be out of a positive concern for the progress of the gospel and the welfare of others.

The teaching of Jesus may have had a wider application than appears from the context. It may have been used as guidance for the missionary activity of the church.

It does, however, have a direct application in the immediate context. We have a responsibility for helping others with their moral struggles. There are times, however, when our attempts may not help. They may result in hostility and the hardening of the sinner. In such cases, it is better not to cast our pearls of spiritual insight before people who are spiritually and psychologically unable to accept them for their worth.

II. On Prayer (Matt. 7:7-12)

Persistence in prayer is essential. It is based upon the confidence that God is a loving Father who will answer prayer.

1. The presuppositions of Christian prayer.   The teaching of Jesus on prayer cannot be understood on the basis of an isolated passage such as this. Jesus did not teach that prayer was a device by which men control God. He did not mean that God will do anything we want him to do if we will just pray long enough.

The presuppositions of all Christian prayers are set forth in the Lord's Prayer. The believer prays to the Father who loves and cares for him. He also prays in the context of the will of God, knowing that only God's will is really good for him.

2. The necessity for persistence in prayer.   But Jesus also taught the necessity for persistence in prayer. The present tense of the Greek verbs permits us to translate: "Keep on asking," "keep on seeking," "keep on knocking."

The lack of persistence in prayer implies a lack of faith in God. When people quit talking to God about their concerns and needs, it is usually because they have lost faith either in God's love or in his capacity. It may even mean that they have ceased to believe that there is a God at all.

Persistence in prayer arises out of a conviction that God loves his child and will answer his prayer by giving him "good things." In his teaching in this passage, Jesus is encouraging just this kind of faith. His argument is from the lesser to the greater. Human fathers with all their faults do not give useless things, such as stones, in answer to their child's cry for bread. They do not give harmful, dangerous things in answer to a plea for fish.

God, a heavenly father who is much greater, wiser, and more loving than earthly fathers, can be trusted to give good things and not evil to his children. It is implicit that he will not grant requests even from his children for things that may be harmful or useless to them.

3. The Golden Rule.   We find the great teaching of Jesus called the Golden Rule appended to his statement about God. God gives and does good for his children. His children are to do good toward others.

Many writers have pointed out that the Golden Rule is found in one form or another in the teachings of various great men. But we find it there in the negative. "Do not do to others what you would not have them do to you."

That is, of course, a good principle. We can agree that we should follow it. But it is hardly the Christian understanding of our responsibility to others. To refrain from doing evil to others is a minimum requirement for peaceful social relationships. But the demand of Jesus goes far beyond this. His followers are to be involved in active, positive, helpful acts of good to others.

III. Two Ways (Matt. 7:13-14)

Jesus contrasts the way of life with the way of destruction.

1. The two gates.   Through the symbols of the contrasting gates, one wide and one narrow, Jesus emphasizes a basic truth. A person does not just stumble by accident onto the way of life. That way is entered by purposeful decision.

Emotion is an important element in religious decision, especially for those of us who are heirs of frontier revivalism. But for Jesus the will is central. Not that emotion is ruled out. But it is not primary. It requires an act of decision and concentration to enter through a narrow gate. The narrow gate to God's salvation is entered in like manner by people who want to enter it, decide to enter it, and concentrate on entering it. Salvation is never a result of chance.

2. The two ways.   The ways correspond to the gates. One is spacious and broad. It requires nothing in terms of commitment and effort. The other is a narrow, tortuous way. It is like one of those winding mountain roads, filled with curves, going dangerously near perilous precipices. One misstep means disaster. You cannot spend time daydreaming or admiring the scenery. You have to concentrate on the path ahead.

Jesus meant by this that the way to which he called men required dedication and discipline. The call to follow Jesus is not the call to an easy life. It is the call to a life of responsible commitment, of constant discipline, of unwavering attention.

3. The two destinies.   The broad way is deceptive in its allurement. It promises ease, freedom from care. It requires nothing in terms of devotion to God, compassionate care for others, self-sacrifice in the service of a heavenly Master. But the people who take this way, expecting a carefree existence without demand or discipline, should be warned about the destiny. The end of the life that flees the discipline of service in love is destruction.

Those who walk the narrow way, however, may rejoice in the prospect awaiting them at the end of the road. They shall find life.

4. The travellers.   The majority spurn the discipline of God's way. People generally prefer the freedom of doing their own thing, of going in the direction in which the desires of the moment lead them. The travellers on the difficult way are few in number. It has always been thus.

This teaching is not given to us, however, so that we can feel smug and secure as members of "the Master's minority." It is not intended to help us determine how many will enjoy heaven with us. No! The teachings of Jesus are not weapons for us to use against others. They confront us with the personal demand of the gospel on our own lives. Whenever we start using them to determine the status of our brother, we have missed their meaning altogether.

IV. False Prophets (Matt. 7:15-20)

Jesus warns against false prophets. He says that they may be known by their fruits. He uses the analogy of goo⁺ ⁺nd bad trees to illustrate the point.

1. The deceptive character of false prophets. The problem is that false prophets cannot be distinguished easily from true prophets on the basis of that which is outward. Their profession is Christian. Their words and deeds have the appearance of genuineness.

It is in the hidden inner character that there is a difference. The outward appearance of the false prophet is contradictory to his character. He is dressed like a sheep, but he is really a ravenous wolf.

2. Known by their fruits. As was often his custom, Jesus used an agricultural metaphor to illustrate his teaching. A sound tree produces good fruit. A tree that is diseased at its heart will produce useless, diseased, or dwarfed fruits. Only at harvesttime could the farmer distinguish the good trees from the unsound ones. Thereupon he cut the bad trees down and burned them.

Does Jesus mean that only at the time of the harvest at the end-time will the quality of fruits be revealed and that then the false prophets will be subject to divine retribution? Or, does he lay upon his followers a responsibility for perceiving the false prophets so that they will not be misled by them?

If the latter is true, what kind of fruits are we to look for? Jesus said that we cannot identify false prophets by their clothing, that is, by their talk and religious acts. In John 10 he talks about true and false shepherds. There the false shepherd is distinguished by his own self-interest and lack of love for the sheep. Perhaps the fruit of the false prophet, therefore, is his willingness to exploit others, his use of religion for his own advantage, his lack of self-giving love.

V. Profession Versus Practice (Matt. 7:15-29)

Jesus teaches that profession must be related to practice. What is important is not what people say but what they do. Only the life that is committed to doing what Christ commands can face the future judgment with assurance. He uses the story of the two foundations to illustrate this teaching.

1. The insufficiency of mere profession. The earliest public Christian confession was the statement by the believer "Jesus is Lord." To say that Jesus is Lord is to acknowledge him as the one into whose service the believer has entered. The analogy is taken from the master-slave relationship. The slave is completely subject to and totally given to the service of his master. This same loyalty is implied in the Christian confession.

In our evangelism we often tell people: "Salvation is easy. All you have to do is trust Christ and confess him." Properly understood, that affirmation is true. But evidently many people do not understand it, thinking that their responsibility ends with that public confession. Our confession of Jesus, however, is but the beginning of a lifetime of service. A profession that does not lead to being and doing what Jesus asks of us is shown by that contradiction to be hypocritical.

2. The inadequacy of religious acts. To prophesy, cast out demons, and perform miraculous deeds—are these not proof-positive that we are genuine followers of Christ, recipients of his power?

Prophecy is the proclamation of divinely communicated truths. These may relate to the past, present, or future. So prophecy in the biblical sense is not to be equated with prediction. People whom we consider emotionally disturbed were among those described as demon-possessed in the ancient world. "Mighty works" would include miracles of healing. To perform such mighty works

in the name of Jesus is to claim him as the source of the insight
or power demonstrated in preaching or miracle-working.

Our day has witnessed a resurgence of interest in exorcism and
healing. Many people claim that miracles are the essential proofs
of the presence, activity, and blessings of the Spirit of God on
his people. But Jesus says: "Not so."

What kind of life, then, demonstrates the reality of our allegiance to Jesus as our Lord? The Sermon on the Mount has
described it. It is not necessarily characterized by a spectacular
series of unusual deeds. More often, it is a life that is lived in
a steady, unassuming, unpublicized way by a person who is filled
with love, mercy, and goodness.

3. *On hearing and doing.*   The audience of Jesus was divided
into two groups. Some were hearers who shrugged off the serious-
ness of his challenges. Perhaps they were intrigued for the moment
and even experienced a fleeting desire to act on what they heard.
They may have even praised him, telling him how much they
enjoyed his talk in the way that people customarily do in our
churches today. But they went away to do nothing. Nothing was
changed. They remained as selfish as they always were, as closed
to God as ever, altering nothing in their life's patterns and goals.

Others, only a few to be sure, took him seriously. They had
been confronted by God's demanding word. That word produced
a crisis in their life. There was repentance and they began to
take the first faltering steps in the new direction dictated by the
compelling insights they had received. They spurned the wide
gate for the narrow, chose the difficult way instead of the easy.

Jesus said that these groups were similar to two men who set
out to build houses. One, the wiser of the two, recognized that
a secure house needed a good foundation. So he chose to build
on a rock. It was not the easiest way, but the wisest course is
often not the easiest. In the time of crisis, his choice was vindicated.
The rains came down, the flood waters rose and swirled around
that house. But they could not wash out that foundation. When
the storm was over, the house was still there.

The other fellow chose a wide, sandy, level place to build his house. It was much easier to work there, and the house went up much more quickly. But in the time of storm when the rain came down, that inviting, level, sandy place became a raging torrent. The dry place was a wadi, which became a river during those infrequent times of heavy rain. The rushing waters ate the sand from under the house, and it fell.

Most interpreters believe that Jesus was talking about the storms of God's final judgment. In that day hypocrisy will be revealed. Empty professions and religious sensationalism will not support the life built on them. Only the life built on the sure foundation of sincere allegiance to Jesus will weather the storm.

Of course, the passage has many applications. Life is filled with storms—defeat, sorrow, disappointment, disillusionment. The person who has real integrity in his discipleship will be able to weather all those storms.

4. The authority of Jesus. The people were accustomed to hearing their teachers quote the sayings of the great rabbis in support of their arguments. But they had been listening to a man who quoted no revered authority of the past. He communicated the word of God in a direct, commanding way. With his own unsupported word, he set aside the traditional opinions assumed to be authoritative. He talked as if there were a direct link between God and himself. The people were amazed by the authority of his word which drew their attention and commanded their respect by its own direct power.

How many of us have read the Sermon on the Mount and felt that same forceful authority? His teachings come to us with an inescapable imperative arising out of their own nature as truth. We know that they are God's word to us and that it is our responsibility to respond to that word.

The statement in verses 28-29 brings the first major section of the gospel to a close. In it we have learned how the gospel story began, and we have heard our Lord's compelling word in the Sermon.

7.
Man of Power and Compassion
8:1 to 9:34

I. Jesus' Authority Over Disease (Matt. 8:1-17)

This passage contains the first of three cycles of miracles found in chapters 8 and 9. Jesus heals a leper, a centurion's servant, and Peter's mother-in-law.

1. The meaning of miracles. There is much misunderstanding today about the continuing role of miracles in the gospel. We must begin by understanding that Jesus was no wandering magician, working miracles indiscriminately to call attention to himself as a mighty miracle-worker.

In the first place, there was no need to convince people in the first century that God could work miracles. They generally believed that anyway. In a recent article a man wrote, "I believe in miracles because I believe in God." Almost anyone in the first century would have been able to say the same thing if Jesus had not ever worked a miracle.

In the second place, the mere fact that Jesus worked miracles did not say anything distinctive about him. People believed that many individuals had the power to work miracles. Great numbers were ready to hail him as a great miracle-worker—one through whom the power of God was expressed in a peculiar way. They followed him in great crowds, attracted by the sensational aspects of his ministry. But—and this is the important thing—they missed the point altogether.

If we are to understand miracles in the Gospels, we must recognize that they played the same role in Jesus' ministry as did his words and other actions. In short, they were vehicles of revelation, intended to show people who Jesus really was. And in order to understand them, one had to look beneath the outward, sensational aspects to see the underlying revelation. The miracles revealed that Jesus was the Son of God, the Savior of all men. Healing the body was secondary. His redemptive mission was primary.

One other word. The gospel is not dependent upon miracles today. We believe that God can and does work miracles. But whether he performs a particular miracle or not has nothing to do with the gospel. If you are ill, it is very important to you to get well. If a loved one is desperately sick, that also is extremely important to you. But whether you or your loved one recovers or dies does not change the gospel a bit. The gospel already exists and is unaffected by contemporary miracles or the lack of them.

2. *The people healed by Jesus.* The people healed by Jesus in this cycle of miracles had one thing in common. All of them, to a greater or lesser degree, were victims of alienation. They were excluded from the main stream of the Jewish community.

The first was a leper. In those days when knowledge of medicine was very primitive indeed, almost any kind of skin disease might be called leprosy. People who suffered from psoriasis, ringworm, rashes caused by emotional disorders, and the like were called lepers. Therefore, we do not know exactly how modern medicine would diagnose the people called lepers in the Bible.

Nonetheless, the leper's plight was a very tragic one. He was excluded from all contact with any but his own kind. It is hard for us to understand the mental and spiritual anguish of the leper in ancient times. He had the feeling that he was a victim of divine displeasure and was even deprived of the support of family and friends.

What Jesus did for the man, therefore, went far beyond the healing of his physical body. He restored him to the community from which he had been excluded. This is probably the key to understanding Jesus' instruction to him, "Go, show yourself to the priest, and offer the gift that Moses commanded." Leviticus 14 contains the procedure for pronouncing a leper clean of his disease so that he could renew his social relationships. Jesus wanted the man to follow that procedure so that he could be reintegrated in society.

What is the meaning of the miracle in terms of the gospel? It is that Jesus is a Savior who overcomes man's alienation and brings him into the community of the redeemed by cleansing him of his sin. Comparatively speaking, there are few lepers that need healing. We can be thankful to God for the modern miracle of medicine that is available to them. But all men are sinners and need a Savior. All men are alienated and need to become a part of a society of acceptance and love.

The second man was the servant of a centurion. A centurion was, technically speaking, the commander of a troop of one hundred men in a Roman legion. However, this centurion was probably in the service of Herod Antipas, since Jesus' ministry at this point is set in Galilee. Nonetheless, he was evidently a Gentile. This was what prompted him to declare himself unworthy to receive Jesus in his home. He was well aware of Jewish traditions that made his home off limits to devout Jews.

So the story deals with a man who has a sense of his own exclusion from Jewish society who comes to Jesus with a deep need. And Jesus meets that need.

Matthew is the most Jewish of all the Gospels. But this is one example of the recognition here in this Gospel of the universality of Christianity. Gentiles also will be included. Indeed, the faith of the centurion prompts Jesus' declaration: "I tell you, many will come from east and west and sit at the table with Abraham, Isaac, and Jacob in the kingdom of God."

There is also the sad recognition that many of the Jews will themselves be excluded: "While the sons of the kingdom will be thrown into outer darkness." The very words of Jesus indicate the real meaning of the miracle. It has to do primarily with salvation rather than with healing.

The third person was a woman, Peter's mother-in-law. Women occupied a very low place in ancient society. Among Jews, a woman's status was very precarious. Her word was no more acceptable in a court of law than that of a slave. If she did not have a man to support her and protect her—a husband, a father, or a son—she was helpless.

But women were important to Jesus and the early church. Because of the gospel, women were able to begin the long, far too slow rise toward a position of dignity and freedom. When Jesus healed her, the woman was able to resume her useful life of service. Is it spiritualizing too much to draw a lesson from this? Through the salvation which Jesus bestows, people are given the possibility of a life of ministry.

3. *The method of healing.* Jesus healed the leper and Peter's mother-in-law by the simple touch of his hand. He did not call upon God. There was no lengthy prayer. He did not use any therapeutic substance in these cases.

Jesus' acts of healings are signs of the presence of the kingdom. In him the power of a sovereign God is fully operative so that there is no secondhand quality to his healings. To perceptive people this aspect of his miracles was the sign that in Jesus, God himself was active among men.

The dialogue with the centurion brings this out sharply. Of all the people who witnessed the ministry of Jesus, the centurion perceived most clearly the truth about his authority.

The centurion was a military man, well acquainted with authority. He responded to the authority of his superiors. All that he needed to act was their word. His own subordinates responded in the same way to his word. This army captain saw in his experience an analogy for understanding the authority of Jesus. But in the case of Jesus, the authority was much more exalted. He commanded the forces that produced illness. All Jesus had to do was to speak, and those forces would obey in the same way that his own soldiers obeyed his command. No wonder Jesus exclaimed: "Not even in Israel have I found such faith!"

4. The theology of the healings.   In his attitude toward disease, Jesus differed sharply from traditional views held by the Jewish people. He did not see disease as an act of God. Rather, it was something that was opposed to God's will for man. Jesus revealed that God was on the side of wholeness and health. His ministry is prophetic of the future of God's people. There will come a day when there shall be no "mourning nor crying nor pain any more, for the former things have passed away" (Rev. 21:4).

II. Jesus' Authority Over Nature, Demons, and Sin (Matt. 8:18 to 9:8)

In this section Jesus confronts two prospective followers with the demands of discipleship. Then the second cycle of miracles is described. Jesus stills a storm, casts demons out of two men, and heals a paralytic.

1. The demands of discipleship.   The first prospective disciple was a volunteer. He vowed to follow Jesus wherever he went. But Jesus perceived that his enthusiasm was superficial. It was based on an erroneous conception of what it meant to be a follower of Jesus.

Perhaps the man was attracted by the popularity of Jesus. The crowds were thronging around him. They were captivated by his words and amazed by his miracles. The unnamed man wanted to be a part of all this. He wanted a share in the excitement and perhaps the glory.

But Jesus' words brought him down to earth: "Foxes have holes, and birds of the air have nests; but the Son of man has nowhere to lay his head." We know that this does not mean that Jesus did not have a place to spend the night. It is even possible that he had his own residence in Capernaum during this phase of his ministry. And he had friends who were glad to receive him.

He was trying to tell this enthusiastic, would-be disciple about the consequences of following him. In the world even the animals had places of security. But it had no place for him. He would not find a hiding place. He was going to be pushed out of his world. We know that this meant that men were going to hunt him down and hang him on a cross. So anyone who wanted to follow him had to be prepared to share that experience with him also.

The second disciple asked for permission to go bury his father. The father was probably an old man whose death could be expected in the relatively near future. One of the duties of a son was to care for his father in his old age and give him an honorable burial. The son wanted to discharge this duty before committing himself to discipleship.

But the responsibility of discipleship must be placed above all other responsibilities. The dead should bury the dead. That is, those who had not received the message of life could take care of this important but secondary task. Men who had heard the gospel of the kingdom needed to bring that gospel of life to men who were spiritually dead.

2. Jesus' authority over nature. Most scholars perceive an ascending order in the miracles described in chapters 8 and 9. In the first cycle of miracles, Jesus had demonstrated his authority over diseases. Now he shows that he is Lord of even greater forces. In this instance also, his authority is expressed in his word. He rebukes the winds and the sea, and they become calm.

The reaction of the disciples is also a point of interest. They respond to the storm with terror, and Jesus rebukes them because of their lack of faith.

Once again, in the life of the church this story had a wider and deeper significance than appears on the surface. Perhaps not many early followers of Jesus ever had an experience just like that of those first disciples. But they all were buffeted by storms of many kinds. Many of them would be engulfed in a storm of persecution. In times like these they, too, would lose their nerve and become terrified. Their faith would be too small.

The story held a lesson for them. No matter how great the storm, Jesus was master of it. The one who calmed the seas could also control the other storms of life.

3. Jesus' authority over demons. Jesus' excursion across the Sea of Galilee took him into the Gentile territory. Gadara was a city five miles southeast of the lake. The district belonging to this city evidently extended to the shore of Galilee. There Jesus encountered two demoniacs who terrorized the populace. Evidently they had seized control of a road which cut through a narrow pass in the mountains and would allow no one to "pass that way."

The main thrust of the story is Jesus' authority over the demonic forces controlling the men. They themselves recognized that authority. They recognized him as their master who had "come before the time." The time referred to is the time when God will exert his sovereign power over the powers of evil, that is, the end-time. In Jesus this sovereign power and authority of God are demonstrated in such a decisive fashion in time that men are forced to reckon with him and are called to repentance while there is yet opportunity.

At the command of Jesus, the demons leave the poor men and are destroyed with the swine in whom they become embodied. The reaction of the inhabitants of the region is one that we would hardly expect. The healing of the demoniacs who had terrorized their neighborhood did not result in gratitude and friendliness. Instead, they rejected Jesus, asking him to leave their territory. This probably resulted from their fear of a person with such power. They saw in him a threat rather than a savior and liberator. The story is an illustration of the rejection with which the gospel would be greeted oftentimes as it was proclaimed in Gentile regions. Many people simply do not want the salvation which Jesus represents for them.

4. The question of demon possession. In the modern religious scene, the question of demon possession has received renewed interest. There is one fact of which we should be aware. Many people who were said to be demon possessed in the first century world would be diagnosed today as emotionally ill.

In the last two thousand years a great deal has been learned about physical and emotional problems which afflict human beings. Thus, most of us pray when we are ill, but we also consult a physician and take prescribed medicines. Most of us will take our emotionally disturbed children to psychiatrists rather than to exorcists.

This is not a contradiction of faith; rather, it can be an expression of faith. We believe in a Creator who is responsible for the resources of healing in our world. And, as Christians, we thank God for all healing, whether it takes place mysteriously and miraculously or whether it takes place through the ministrations of a physician.

In the first century, the emphasis was on the spiritual aspects of the human predicament. This is a truth that modern medicine, including psychiatry, has largely missed. The power of evil over the lives of people has been ignored.

The devil, demons, the world, the flesh—these are terms used in the New Testament to describe the power or powers to which man is often a helpless victim. One major aspect of the gospel is its affirmation that the salvation which comes through Jesus Christ liberates from all evil powers which tyrannize us.

The role of the preacher in primitive societies today is analagous to the role of the Christian witness in the first century. It would be a mistake for him to tell people who live in mortal fear of evil powers and spirits: "I have come to liberate you by getting rid of all your superstitious fears through a process of education." Rather, he should proclaim the truth of the gospel: "The power of Jesus to save you is greater than the power of the spirits that hold you in bondage."

The primary duty of the preacher of the gospel is not to argue about the terminology which may be in vogue in any given culture. Instead, it is his privilege to proclaim to all people: "The power of the gospel is greater than any power that holds you in bondage, however you may describe that power."

Through his exorcisms of demons, Jesus demonstrated that he had sovereign authority over the power of evil which enslaves people. It should be noticed once again that his authority was expressed in his word. His approach to exorcisms was vastly different to the ritual portrayed in the film *The Exorcist.*

5. *Jesus' authority to forgive sins.*   The story of the paralytic is an unusual one. It demonstrates clearly the recognition on Jesus' part that there is a close connection between spiritual and physical health. The man was paralyzed, and that was a grievous problem. But he had another problem even more serious—his sin and guilt. Jesus addressed himself to this serious problem. In pronouncing the man forgiven, Jesus once again was revealing who he was. He was taking on himself the authority to which God alone had a right—the authority to forgive sin.

His audience recognized what he had done and reacted sharply to it. They accused Jesus of blasphemy. They refused to see who Jesus was. He was Immanuel, God with us. He was the King Messiah who possessed the prerogative to forgive sins.

As Jesus implied, it is easier from one point of view to pronounce a man's sins forgiven than to tell a paralytic to walk. If his words had no healing effect, the spectators could easily verify that. It would be impossible, however, for them to decide on an objective basis if his sins had actually been forgiven. They would have to accept the objective healing miracle, therefore, as proof of his power to forgive sins.

This story simply underlines the truth that we have emphasized. The important thing is not whether people believed that Jesus could heal. They had no problem accepting the possibility of miracle workers. But, if they did not recognize Jesus as the Savior and forgiver of men's sins, they failed to see the truth of God's revelation in the miracle.

6. Son of man. The title "Son of man" (9:6) was Jesus' favorite designation of himself. Perhaps he used this title instead of "Messiah" because of the connotations of the latter. The Jews expected a Messiah who would be a national deliverer and who would reestablish the rule of Israel. When they heard the word "Messiah," they associated these ideas with it.

The title "Son of man" goes back to Daniel 7:13. It also appears in the book of Enoch, a noncanonical Jewish book dated about 200 B.C. The Son of man is a figure of power and glory expected to appear in the end-time. Jesus uses this title but reinterprets it. The Son of man must suffer and die (see Matt. 16:21-28). This means that the path to glory and power leads through suffering and rejection.

III. Jesus' Authority Over Death (Matt. 9:9-34)

This section begins with two controversies. First, there is the controversy with the Pharisees over Jesus' acceptance of tax collectors and sinners. Next, Jesus answers the criticism brought by disciples of John against the failure of his followers to fast. A third cycle of miracles follows these controversies. Jesus heals a woman who suffers from chronic hemorrhage, raises a ruler's daughter from the dead, and heals two blind men and a mute.

1. The friend of tax collectors and sinners. Matthew, the tax collector, was probably in the service of Herod Antipas, the ruler of Galilee. Evidently his post was in Capernaum where he levied tribute on commerce passing along the road from Damascus to Acre. He may have been responsible for taxing fishing and other industry in the region.

Tax collectors were a despised group among the Jews. They were often unscrupulous, enriching themselves at the expense of their countrymen by exorbitant charges, a part of which they

kept for themselves. By calling Matthew and by his association
with people like him, Jesus cut across the grain of social prejudices.

The fact that he ate with tax collectors and sinners enraged
many of his fellow Jews. The sinners were the common people
who did not follow the religious traditions of the Pharisees. They
were not necessarily immoral people, as judged by our standards.
If they did not observe the purification rules, as, for example,
washing their hands before eating, they were classed as sinners.

The freedom of Jesus for people is one of the outstanding
characteristics of his ministry. No one was outside the pale for
him. He was ready to associate with any human being, no matter
how he was classified by society and no matter how much he
was ostracized by his fellows. But when one identifies with people
who are despised by society, he must be willing to be rejected
by that society.

Jesus' answer to the criticism of the self-righteous is tinged with
irony. "Those who are well" and "the righteous" was probably
uttered with a great deal of sarcasm. The "sick" are the tax
collectors and sinners gathered around Jesus in humble gratitude
because of his gracious acceptance of them.

The religious leaders needed to learn the meaning of their own
Scriptures which they claimed to follow. The great prophet Hosea
had expressed the desire of God in a statement that they ignored.
"I desire mercy, and not sacrifice" (Hos. 6:6). The Pharisees
thought that they would gain the favor of God by their scrupulous
observance of religious ritual. But they had only become self-righteous in the process, despising and excluding people whom God
in his mercy accepted.

2. *The question of fasting.* Fasting is mentioned frequently
in the Old Testament. But it is generally of a spontaneous kind,
connected with great crisis and sorrow and accompanied by other
signs of mourning. The only annual fast in pre-exilic Judaism was
in connection with the Day of Atonement (Lev. 16:29,31, etc.).
Fasting was understood to be a fulfillment of the command to

the people to afflict themselves (see also the cor
6:16-18).

Jesus himself fasted, according to the Gospels. I
of the type mentioned in the Old Testament. They were a spontaneous response to a moment of crisis. Jesus evidently did not adopt
the custom of regular fasts, neither did he ask his disciples to
observe the prevailing religious practice. The disciples of John
the Baptist could not understand this, for to them fasting was
one mark of a religious person.

Jesus' answer reveals his concept of fasting. For his disciples
to fast at the moment would be inappropriate. There was no
occasion for it. He was still with them, and their fellowship was
characterized by joy. In the dark days that lay ahead, however,
there would be sorrow and a sense of loss. Fasting in those circumstances would be an expression of their mourning. In other words,
fasting has meaning only if it is a spontaneous, free response to
a particular situation and not as a religious ritual.

People like John's disciples were trying to make the new,
dynamic force that was being released in the ministry of Jesus
fit into the old religious forms of Judaism. Jesus used two illustrations to show why this would not work. People did not patch
an old garment with a piece of unshrunk cloth. Should they do
so, their folly would show up the first time they washed the
patched garment. Neither did they put new wine into old, rigid
wineskins, because the new wine in the process of fermentation
and expansion would burst the old skins. In the same manner,
the gospel of Jesus could not be put into the old forms of Judaism
without disastrous results.

3. The third cycle of miracles. Most interpreters believe that
the three cycles of miracles contained in Matthew 8-9 reach their
climax in the story about the healing of the ruler's daughter. The
ruler is identified in the Markan parallel as "one of the rulers
of the synagogue" named Jairus (Mark 5:22). The ruler of the
synagogue was responsible for the physical arrangements for the

services.

In the first group of miracles, we saw that Jesus demonstrated his authority over disease. In the second group, he showed himself to be sovereign over nature and demons. Now he shows that he is master of death.

The message for the Christian community is clear. Jesus not only had the power to bring someone back to physical life; he is also the resurrection and the life. All Christians face death. Our hope is not that a miracle will be performed to bring us back to this life. Our hope is that the Sovereign Lord of death and life will raise us to life eternal.

4. The reactions to Jesus. The purpose of the last miracle in this cycle (9:32-34) is primarily to show the two-fold reaction to Jesus' ministry. When he cured the mute, the crowds were amazed. They recognized that no one had ever done the things that Jesus had done in the history of their nation.

The religious leaders could not deny the reality of the miracles performed by Jesus. So they attempted to destroy his influence by raising suspicions about the source of his power. They claimed that it came from the devil, the prince of demons.

Sometimes when the gospel is preached, people will say: "There were no decisions today. We did not see any response." But there is always response to the gospel. Sometimes the response is the desired one; people accept the message of salvation. But if the response is not positive, it is negative. We should not be surprised at this, for this pattern has existed from the very beginning of Christian history. People did not always make the choice which Jesus himself desired them to make. More often than not they decided against him.

8.
Sheep Among Wolves
9:35 to 10:42

I. The Need for Laborers (Matt. 9:35 to 10:4)

The crowds evoke Jesus' compassion, for he sees them as helpless sheep without shepherds. He instructs his disciples to pray to the Father for laborers to gather in the harvest represented by the crowds. Thereupon, he summons the twelve and endues them with authority for this task.

1. The condition of the sheep. Sheep are notoriously helpless creatures, totally dependent on their shepherd for protection against wild animals like wolves. Without such care they are harassed by their natural enemies and unable to find the scarce vegetation upon which their lives depend in arid regions.

The metaphor "sheep without a shepherd" was a well-known figure of speech in the Old Testament for a leaderless people. In Numbers 27:17 God instructs Moses to choose Joshua as his successor "that the congregation of the Lord may not be as sheep which have no shepherd." It is also found in the gloomy prophecy of Micaiah about the projected campaign planned by Ahab and Jehoshaphat against Syria (1 Kings 22:17).

There were numerous people in Israel who claimed to be religious leaders. But instead of protecting and nourishing the sheep, more often than not they preyed upon them. They were wolves instead of shepherds. Or, they abandoned the people, despising them because of their lack of attention to the religious traditions and practices accepted and promulgated by the Pharisees and others. By their self-righteous exclusivism or by their exploitation of people, religious leaders betray the shepherd role.

How different was the attitude of Jesus! He loved the abandoned, helpless, harassed multitudes. He had the shepherd heart.

2. Laborers for the harvest.   Jesus recognized that the people, hungry and disoriented, were like a field ready for the harvest. They would respond to the message of God's salvation and love. But the task was so great. The people were many; the laborers few. He needed help to lead them into the care of the great Shepherd.

He called upon his disciples, therefore, to pray for the Lord of the harvest to send the laborers adequate for so great a harvest. At least three great truths are seen in this request. First, God is the Lord of the harvest. Jesus recognized that God was the one to whom the harvest belonged and that its success depended totally upon him. God would bring the harvest about.

Second, Jesus taught that God would bring about the harvest through laborers. Christian disciples have the great privilege of being laborers in God's field. They have a unique and essential role to play in God's redemptive work. People are brought to salvation by God's message of salvation. But they cannot hear the message unless it is proclaimed by loyal workers.

Third, the laborers must be sent forth by God. God calls men and women to help in the work of the harvest. The initiative in redemption lies with God from beginning to end. His word is the gospel of salvation. It is proclaimed by men and women whom he chooses and whom he sends forth to labor for him.

3. The first of the laborers.   Jesus himself took the initiative in meeting the need for laborers. As God's representative, he made the selection of the first missionaries to be sent out to the field. He it was who called them. He it was who provided them with the resources for their task. They were given the same authority that he had exercised—the authority to cast out demons and heal the sick.

The choice of twelve apostles in itself is significant to our

understanding of the mission of Jesus. The word apostle means
"one who is sent out." It was sometimes used in the same way
that we use the word *missionary* (see, e.g., Acts 14:4,14; Rom.
16:7).

But these twelve occupy a special place in the history of redemption. They were twelve specially chosen representatives of
Jesus himself. They were his helpers, commissioned to help him
complete his own task of calling Israel to repentance in view
of the decisive moment which his presence represented. Their
message was to be the same one which he had proclaimed. Their
activities were to be an extension of the activities in which he
had been engaged. No other group of missionaries in Christian
history has ever had the precise role which was given to the
twelve for that mission to Israel during Jesus' ministry. As his
representatives, endued with his authority, proclaiming his message, they were to be a sign to Israel that the messianic age had
dawned and that the one who sent them was none other than
the promised Messiah.

Twelve were chosen in an act that symbolized Israel in its
totality. The choice of the twelve was a declaration that the
purpose of Jesus was to constitute the New Israel of God by calling
out of the old Israel the saved remnant, characterized by its
responsiveness to God's Messiah. The ultimate purpose of God
as seen in both the Old and New Testaments is not to save
individual souls. God's redemptive purpose is to create a people,
his own people who respond to him in love and obedience. The
individual who claims to be saved but who has not been identified
with God's people, the church, has at the very least aborted the
purpose of God for his own life.

That small group, the nucleus of the new Israel, was at best
a very unlikely group with which to begin the process of creating
the people of God. No doubt, any one of us would have chosen
different kinds of people. We would have looked in the upper
classes for the best educated, most talented, and most promising

young men we could find.

A number of the twelve were fishermen. The most prominent of these was Simon. Jesus gave him another name. It was Cephas in Aramaic, the native language of the disciples. In Greek, it was Petros. Both these words mean "rock," but we call him Peter, an anglicized form of his Greek name.

Another of the disciples was a tax collector, a member of a group despised and hated by their fellow Jews. Another was also named Simon. He is called "the Canaanean," which should probably be understood as "the zealot." Evidently he was a member of the radical revolutionary Jewish party that preached the overthrow of the Roman rule by military revolt. And, of course, Judas Iscariot was a traitor to his master, the first of a long, tragic list of people who, instead of serving faithfully in the harvest, have failed to live up to the expectation of their Lord.

II. Instructions for the Laborers (Matt. 10:5-15)

Jesus gives instructions to the twelve concerning the area of their mission, their message and activities, and their equipment for the journey. He tells them how they are to respond to acceptance and rejection of their mission.

1. The mission and message of the twelve.   Jesus defined the area of his disciples' responsibility very narrowly. They were not to go to the Gentiles, that is, into the region of Syria to the north or Decapolis to the east. They were to enter no town of Samaria, which lay to the south of Galilee. They were to confine their efforts to Jews in Galilee itself.

This fact is somewhat disturbing at first glance. Was Jesus not as concerned about Gentiles as he was about Jews? The answer of the New Testament is that he was and that he himself laid the foundation for the inclusion of the Gentiles. However, in God's plan of redemption it was necessary for Jesus to call Israel to repentance first. God intended the gospel to go from the Jew to the Gentile. The foundations had to be laid among the Jews.

But the temple erected on the foundation would include people from all the nations.

The message of the twelve was the same as that proclaimed by Jesus. In fact, as they went forth, it was as though he was going forth. They were simply multiplying his efforts. They were to proclaim that the moment of decision had arrived for Israel. This moment of decision was produced by the coming of the kingdom of God, the manifestation of God's kingly rule. The sovereign power of God was expressed in the teachings, exorcisms, and healings performed by Jesus and now by his disciples as his representatives.

2. *The equipment and support of the twelve.* Jesus cautioned his disciples against using the gospel for personal financial advantage. They had paid nothing for the great gift they had received from God. Their relationship to Jesus was based upon grace, the unmerited favor of God. They were not to use that which had come to them as a gift for personal profit.

Unscrupulous people have found that religion can be very profitable. If I can convince people that I have a secret from God or that I have some power to heal them or save them, I am in a position to exercise great control over them. I can barter my secret or my power for position, prestige, and money. This cheapens and distorts the Christian gospel, which is not for sale. It should not be used to amass personal fortune or great personal power.

On the other hand, Jesus told the disciples that they were to depend upon the recipients of their message for their livelihood during the mission. They were advised to take no money or provisions for the trip. They were to go out completely dependent on the people who responded to their message. The principle is: "The laborer deserves his food."

The apostle Paul refers to this teaching of Jesus (1 Cor. 9:11). He understood that the support of the ministry arises out of the nature of the church as a fellowship (Gal. 6:6). The Christian community is based upon the concept of mutual sharing. No person can give himself totally to the ministry of the gospel for very long without receiving the essentials for his life. He shares with the people what he has, his life, talents, and service. They, in turn, share with him what they have, in order that he may carry on his ministry.

Jesus instructed his disciples to take no more than was absolutely essential by way of equipment. They were not even to take a change of clothes or shoes. The tunic was the inner garment or undershirt worn beneath the cloak.

One of the reasons for this was the urgency of the mission. They were to visit the towns as rapidly as possible and so needed to be unencumbered by baggage.

3. *The relation of the twelve to the hearers.* Jesus gave his disciples instructions about how they were to comport themselves once they reached a town. First, they were to discover by enquiries who was worthy in it. "Worthy" in this context probably means someone who has a good reputation and is esteemed by his fellow townsmen. This was simply commonsense advice. In this rapid mission through the towns of Galilee, it was essential for the messengers to assure the best immediate hearing for their gospel. Association with disreputable persons would doom their mission from the outset.

"Let your peace come upon the house" refers to the usual Semitic greeting "shalom" or "peace." Peace in the Old Testament was often the practical equivalent of salvation. And in this instance, the greeting by the disciples stood for the peace of the Messiah, or the messianic salvation of the last days.

If, however, the messenger and this greeting met with hostility and rejection, the inhabitants of that household would not receive the blessings of God's peace through his Messiah. In such a case, the disciples were to "shake off the dust from their feet." This was an act often performed by a Jew as he returned to Palestine after traveling through pagan lands. He would shake off the contaminating dust of impure regions. When the disciples shook the dust of hostile towns off their feet, they were actually saying that these Jewish settlements were as pagan lands. Having rejected God's call to repentance, they themselves were rejected by God. His judgment awaited them—a judgment in which their punishment would be more severe than that meted out to Sodom and Gomorrah, which were proverbial for their wickedness.

We should note here that the instructions of Jesus were for this particular, urgent mission. The time was short. The time of Messiah's presence among his people would soon end. The need to reach as many of the Jewish people as possible was urgent. In later missions, the Christian church rightly has not ceased her attempts to reach peoples who have been hostile to the gospel initially.

III. The Peril Facing the Missionaries (Matt. 10:16-33)

Jesus warns his disciples of the persecution that faces them. He tells them not to fear their persecutors. They have power only over the physical life, but God's power extends beyond this. He determines the eternal fate of the individual. Moreover, they can trust in his love and care for each one of them. Therefore, they are to openly confess Jesus before a hostile world, knowing that he will acknowledge them before the heavenly Father. In this section, as is his wont, Matthew has brought together materials on discipleship that are found in various places in Mark and Luke. Some of Jesus' sayings, therefore, apply not only to the disciples' mission to Israel but also to the wider Christian mission to a Gentile world.

1. Inevitable persecution. The situation of the disciples in an evil world is a precarious and helpless one. They are to be in the world as Jesus was in the world. This means that their lives will be characterized by vulnerability. They will be sheep among wolves. Not only does this metaphor depict the vulnerability of the disciples, it also implies something about their reaction to their enemies. They are not to respond to hostility and persecution with the weapons used by the world. Rather than strike back, they are to turn the other cheek.

At the same time, they are not to be thoughtless and foolishly expose themselves to danger. They are to be wise as serpents. They are to use all the resources of their intelligence in dealing with a hostile, oppressive society. When the situation appears hopeless, they are even to resort to flight in order to be able to continue their ministry in other towns.

They will be brought before councils. These councils are the local sanhedrins or Jewish courts that functioned in the synagogue. One of the common punishments meted out by the courts was flogging, which could not exceed 39 strokes. Paul says: "Five times I have received at the hands of the Jews the forty lashes less one" (2 Cor. 11:24).

The disciples would also be dragged before governors, Roman officials like Pontius Pilate, and kings, the petty kings like Herod Antipas.

Jesus' followers are not to worry about their defense in these situations. When they are brought to trial, they will not stand before their accusers and judges alone. The Spirit of the Father will be with them. He will help them respond to the accusations levelled against them.

One of the most difficult of all experiences to be confronted by the disciples is the enmity and persecution from their own family. Many times in Christian history, believers have found that parents, children, and brothers turned against them when they became followers of Jesus.

2. *Difficult sayings.* Matthew 10:22-23 contains statements which present some difficulties for the interpreter. Jesus declares that the disciples will be hated "for his name's sake." This means that they will be hated because they are his followers, identified with him, and committed to his service.

But Jesus promised: "He who endures to the end will be saved." The word *saved* in the New Testament may refer to the experience of conversion, to the present activity of God in the life of the believer, or to the future victory of the Christian over sin and death. The latter is the meaning here. The believer who is faithful through all the difficulties and persecutions resulting from his loyalty to Jesus will be vindicated in the last judgment.

The second difficult statement is Jesus' prediction that the Son of man will come before the disciples have evangelized all the towns of Israel. The interpreter must make a choice between two major possibilities. We may take the statement literally. Jesus predicted the end of the age with the coming in glory of the Son of man before the disciples had completed the mission to Israel upon which he was sending them. This would mean that Jesus was mistaken in his prediction, since the end did not come.

The other choice is to identify the coming of the Son of man with some manifestation of his power and glory other than with his glorious appearance at the end-time. We can be sure of one thing. The writer of the Gospel did not understand this statement as a mistaken prediction made by Jesus, or he would not have included it in his writing.

How then can we understand the coming of the Son of man mentioned in this passage by Jesus? Many have associated it with the transfiguration described in chapter 17. Still others have suggested the resurrection or Pentecost. Perhaps the transfiguration in which the glory of Jesus was revealed to his disciples best fulfills the demands of the text. It occurred before Jesus and his messengers had completed their mission to the towns of Israel.

IV. The Divisive Gospel (Matt. 10:34-42)

Jesus tells his disciples that following him may cause their own family to turn against them. But they must be faithful to him even at the cost of their own lives. He promises to reward those who befriend his followers.

1. The inevitability of alienation.   The purpose of God in
the incarnation was reconcilation. This is the central teaching
of the New Testament. Jesus came to overcome the barriers which
separate men from God and reconcile them to him. Not only
so, he came to deal with the problems of hostility, greed, and
prejudice which divide men from one another and bring them
together in a new relationship as brothers and sisters, members
of God's own family. Indeed, these two works of reconciliation
are one and the same. Men who enter into a right relation with
God also enter into a right relation with one another.

But the establishment of a new relationship often raises a threat
to old ones. This is true in human affairs. Jonathan's friendship
with David caused tensions between him and his father. When
a man marries, he may find that his commitment to his wife has
a divisive effect on his relationship with his parents.

This is true, of course, only when the new commitment is
interpreted as a rejection of the old. Marriage need not divide
a person from his parents. It will do so only if their claims on
him rival the claims of his wife.

And so it is with the Christian life. Commitment to Christ does
not necessarily shatter the old family ties. It does so, however,
when the family demands renunciation of the claims of Christ
as the price for their good will. The choice may be this: You
must choose between your faith and your family.

To be sure, Jesus does not will that family reject his disciples
because they are his disciples. On the other hand, he does will
that men remain true to him no matter what the cost. If the
choice is forced upon a believer, he must choose Christ rather
than his family.

This passage comes to grips with one of the harshest, most
painful realities of Christian experience. To see those whom you
love turn against you, to see their love turn to hate, and to have
them treat you as an enemy is one of the severest tests that any

Christian can endure. Many of those earliest followers of Jesus had to face exactly this test. And since that time, many others have read this passage, not as abstract theory but as the painful demand of the gospel upon them in the concrete situations of their life.

In such situations Jesus did not come to bring peace. He will not allow the decision that will enable family ties to remain as they were. He came to bring a sword. The tie must be severed. The believer must accept rejection by the family in order to remain true to his Lord.

Not only so. He must be willing to walk the way of the cross completely. He must be faithful to Jesus and his will no matter what the price society may exact, whether it be rejection, persecution, or death itself.

The concern of the disciple is not for his own welfare. He is not to retreat in a cowardly attempt to save himself. Ironically, the person who is devoted to self-preservation will lose his life. He may avoid the threat of the moment. He may find temporary safety in yielding to the pressures of an evil society. But he cannot guarantee his life. Sooner or later his efforts will be in vain. No matter how much he strives for his own security, he will be frustrated ultimately, for he will die.

On the other hand, the person who follows Jesus without regard to personal safety will find his life. His concern is not his own security but the service of God. When his commitment to the Lord leads him into personal danger, he chooses to die rather than be unfaithful. But the God whom he serves guarantees his future. He can be confident, therefore, that he will find life.

2. *The promise to friends of the disciples.* Some will reject and persecute Jesus' followers. Others, however, will befriend them and identify with them. In order to understand the force of Jesus' words in this connection, we must understand the context to which they speak.

The teachings of Jesus presuppose a situation in which his disciples are scorned by society and are objects of its hatred. Their existence in such a society is a precarious one, to say the least. To befriend believers in these circumstances by opening one's home to them and giving them aid and comfort requires an inordinate amount of courage. When a person identifies with another who is scorned and rejected by society, he himself becomes an object of that same malice.

Receiving the messenger sent out by Jesus has a consequence that goes far beyond the obvious. When the disciples of Jesus went out under his authority, it was as though Jesus himself was going out in their person. People who received the messengers, therefore, were in effect receiving Jesus who sent them out. Jesus, however, had been sent by God and represented him. To receive Jesus was tantamount to receiving God.

The person who opens heart and home to the prophet, God's messenger, is promised the prophet's reward. That is, his blessings from God will be the same as the blessings the prophet will receive. The same is true of the one who receives the righteous man. A righteous man in the context of the gospel is the one who is committed to the way of life demanded by Jesus.

Furthermore, giving a cup of cold water to a little one brings its reward from God. "Little one" means an obscure, unimportant member of the Christian community. A cup of cold water stands for the minimum gesture of hospitality and friendliness. Therefore, the one who performs the smallest service for the most insignificant child of God may be assured that his act will not go unnoticed by God.

9.

Shall We Look for Another?

11:1-30

I. Jesus and John the Baptist (Matt. 11:1-19)

From prison a troubled John sends messengers to ask Jesus
if he is the Coming One. Jesus replies by pointing to his
life-giving and healing miracles and to his proclamation of
the gospel as the evidence of his identity. Subsequently Jesus
affirms the greatness of John and describes his relation to
God's plan of redemption. He criticizes the popular attitude
toward John and himself.

1. John's problem. John had been in prison since the beginning
of Jesus' Galilean ministry. He had been placed by Herod Antipas
in the military stronghold of Machaerus, located in the extreme
southern part of Perea near the Dead Sea. Antipas, who ruled
over Galilee and Perea, wanted to get him as far from the center
of things as possible in order to counteract his influence with
the people. According to Josephus, the first-century Jewish historian, Herod believed that John threatened the stability of his
kingdom because of his popularity with the people. The Gospels
tell us that the immediate cause of John's arrest had been his
denunciation of the illicit union between Antipas and Herodias,
his brother's wife.

While John was in prison, reports kept coming to him about
Jesus' activities. They were not at all what he expected. He had
predicted that the coming Messiah would lay the ax to the root
of the trees, that he would bring God's judgment upon evil men
and save the righteous. But that had not happened at all. Evil

still ran its unchecked course. He was in jail with an uncertain future, while the evil Herod was still on his throne. And Rome still had an unshakable grip on Israel. Apparently nothing had been changed by the coming of Jesus. Had John been mistaken? One wonders what a chapter about this period from an autobiography of John would reveal. What doubts? What fears?

John, therefore, decided to send some of his followers to Jesus to find out if Jesus was in fact the Messiah. It is interesting that he asked Jesus himself to answer his doubts. This says a great deal about John's confidence in Jesus' integrity.

Jesus answered John's question by pointing to the kinds of things he was doing—healing the blind, lame, deaf; raising the dead; preaching the gospel to the poor. These were the kinds of things that Isaiah had talked about as signs of the coming age (see Isa. 35:4-6; 61:1). In effect, Jesus was telling John that his messianic expectations were wrong. He, along with other Jews, had erroneous ideas about the kind of work the Messiah would do. They were looking for a victorious conqueror and an avenger of evil, but they needed to reevaluate their ideas in the light of Isaiah's insights.

Jesus concluded his remarks to John's disciples with the statement: "Blessed is he who takes no offense at me." The verb translated "takes offense" usually has the meaning "to stumble or fall into sin." The blessed man, therefore, is the one who is open to the revelation of God in Jesus and who is not caused to stumble into the sin of rejecting it because Jesus does not fit his preconceived notions of what the Messiah is to do.

2. The greatness of John. The crowds may have gotten the wrong idea about John from his question. They may have thought that he had lost his nerve and had become a weak, vacillating man. But Jesus assured them that this was not so. They had not made the trip into the desert to see a reed shaking in the wind, that is, a weak, cowardly man, influenced by the changing winds of public pressure and opinion. They had not gone to see a soft

sycophant interested in social position and wealth. Had this been
their purpose, they would have gone to the royal courts where
people with those interests flocked together. They had been attracted to John during his ministry because he was a strong,
courageous prophet of God. And they had been correct in their
estimate of John. He was indeed a prophet, God's spokesman
who challenged the evil of his day and called men to repentance.
Furthermore, John had not changed. He was still the undaunted
prophet they had seen in the desert.

3. *John's place in God's plan of redemption.* But John was
more than a prophet. He was that special messenger described
in Malachi 3:1. He was the forerunner whose ministry signaled
the nearness of Messiah's appearance. He was the Elijah of Jewish
messianic expectation. In terms of his character, his commitment
to God, and the courage of his ministry, no greater man than
John had ever been born. But there is a paradox in this description
of John the Baptist. He who is least in the kingdom is greater
than John.

Some interpreters have understood the "least in the kingdom"
as a reference to Jesus himself. He is apparently small, insignificant,
unrecognized. He is certainly not the national hero, come to satisfy
Israel's desires for freedom and power. But he is greater than
the great John. Perhaps this is the meaning.

But most interpreters understand Jesus' enigmatic statement
differently. John is great; there is none greater in human terms.
But, as great as he was, he belonged to the old age, the age
of the prophets. He stood right at the dividing line. It was his
privilege to announce the dawn of the new age. But he was not
a part of that age. The least of the followers of Jesus is greater
than John, not in terms of personal character and achievement
but in terms of privilege. Each Christian is an actual participant
in the age of which John was the forerunner. He has the good
fortune to be a disciple of Jesus.

Verse 12 contains a very difficult statement that has been

variously interpreted. What did Jesus mean when he said that "the kingdom of heaven has suffered violence, and men of violence take it by force"? Most probably Jesus was referring to the violent opposition by evil men to God's rule that had come among men in Jesus. That violence had begun with John the Baptist. Even then God's great prophet, the herald of the kingdom, lay in Antipas' prison cell. And vicious men were working and plotting at that moment to bring about the downfall of Jesus.

4. The people's reaction to the ministries of John and Jesus. The people had shown themselves to be fickle and arbitrary in their attitude toward John and Jesus. Jesus illustrated their unreasonable attitude by comparing them to children at play. Some children want to play "wedding." But when they play the joyous wedding music, their playmates refuse to dance. Others want to play "funeral." But when they wail, the others do not join in the mourning. They want to determine the game to be played and force their companions to join in on their terms.

People had not been willing to accept John and Jesus as they were. John was a stern, ascetic wilderness prophet. Gripped with a sense of the crisis of the moment, he found very little to laugh about. He held himself aloof from the common life. The people did not like that forbidding aloofness. They wanted to play "wedding," but John refused to dance. So they said that he "had a demon." This meant that they thought he was crazy.

Jesus was the opposite. He was a participant in social functions, a guest at weddings and banquets. But the people did not like that either. They especially did not like his propensity to socialize with tax collectors and sinners. They wanted to play "funeral" with Jesus, but he would not cooperate. So they called him "a glutton and a drunkard," an exaggeration as such criticisms usually are. They resented the fact that neither of the two men fitted into their mold. But it was evident from the contradiction in their attitudes that neither John nor Jesus could have pleased them, no matter what they had done.

So many times we miss God's word to us simply because it comes in unexpected ways that contradict our notions. If the gospel teaches us anything about God at all, it teaches that we cannot put him in a mold. He must be free to act in the way that he chooses. Man's responsibility is to be open to his actions and sensitive to his word so that he does not miss the message of God because it comes to him in unwanted ways.

But God's wisdom in acting through John and Jesus is justified by what he accomplished. This seems to be the meaning of the difficult statement: "Yet wisdom is justified by his deeds." In order for God to achieve his purpose of redemption, he needed two men totally different from one another to fill two different roles.

II. The Rejection of Jesus (Matt. 11:20-30)

Jesus pronounces a series of woes on the cities located at the focal point of his Galilean ministry. Though some have rejected him, others have received his revelation of God. Jesus invites the weary and burdened to come to him.

1. Unrepentant cities. The center of Jesus' ministry during this period was Capernaum on the northwest shore of the Sea of Galilee. Bethsaida was located on the north shore, and Chorazin lay a little more than two miles north-northwest of Capernaum. Here it was that Jesus had been performing his mighty works and calling people to repentance. But the presence of Jesus had not produced the desired results.

Of course, he had been exceedingly popular with large numbers of people. They had flocked to hear him and to see what he would do. But their response to Jesus was at best a superficial one. Jesus did not desire to be a sensational hero. He wanted people to turn to God, and there had been very little of that.

Opportunity implied responsibility. Because God had given to them his greatest revelation, their situation at the judgment would be worse than that of Tyre and Sidon, the Gentile cities of Phoenicia. Jesus was convinced that Tyre and Sidon would have come to repentance had his ministry been directed toward them. The fact is that Gentile peoples in later times were to prove more responsive to the gospel than was Jesus' own nation to him during his ministry.

The problem was arrogance. In their pride, the people of those rebellious cities had refused to accept God's message to them. They had refused to repent—to turn from their own way to submit to the rule of God. Filled with a false sense of their importance, they thought that they would receive God's approval on the basis of their own merit. But the exact opposite was the case. Instead of being exalted to heaven, they would be brought down to hades, the shadowy underworld of departed spirits.

2. Receptive children. Children or "babes" is a figure used by Jesus for those people who respond to his call for repentance and humbly turn to God, accepting his rule. "Babes" is in contrast to the arrogant people in those cities which had rejected Jesus' ministry. The arrogant person in the Bible is the man who thinks that he does not need God, who trusts in his own wisdom, who depends on his own resources. The humble person, or babe, is one who recognizes his own limitations and needs and who humbly depends solely on God.

The passage (11:25-27) in which Jesus sets forth the relationship of the Son to the Father, on the one hand, and to believers, on the other, is often called the Johannine passage because of its obvious similarity in thought and language to the Gospel of John.

According to God's will, as perceived by Jesus, a relationship to God cannot be achieved through human effort. It can only come through revelation, God-given insight. Furthermore, the focal point of that revelation is the person of Jesus, the incarnate Son. He is the key to God's redemptive activity.

The Son, and the Son alone, knows the Father. This is not intellectual knowledge but the knowledge of a relationship. The Son knows the Father because of the unique intimacy of his relationship with him. No one else can come directly to this knowledge of God.

But, according to the divine purpose of redemption, the Son had come into the world in order to make the Father known to men. When the believer enters into relationship with the Son, he also enters into a relationship with the Father. In other words, he comes to "know" God in the bibilical sense.

In none of this is human effort or planning determinative. The Son reveals the Father to those whom he chooses. In salvation the initiative is with God. He must take the first step.

The doctrine of predestination is a wonderful concept unless it is perverted. Some people have believed that God wills the damnation of the lost just as he wills the salvation of the redeemed. This is unacceptable to most of us. It contradicts the basic revelation of the New Testament about God: that he is a God of love and his love goes out equally to all men. But predestination means that our salvation depends upon God first and last. We are saved, not because we reached out to God, but because he reached out to us. We can have great security about our salvation because we trust in him to finish the work begun in us.

In this passage, therefore, two great truths are apparent. First, men who are saved owe their salvation to the fact that God reached out to them. Second, arrogant men cannot be saved. Salvation is for children who, humbly aware of their own needs, gratefully and joyously accept God's gift to them through the Son.

3. *The great invitation.* Appropriately enough, this section in which Jesus has addressed the two groups who have responded in opposite ways to his call for repentance ends with a poignant invitation. God's call goes out through Jesus. The invitation is to those who are "weary and heavy laden." These words describe persons who have been trying to make it on their own. They have been following the religious prescriptions of their leaders. In an effort to please God, they have been attempting to live by the laws contained in the great mass of oral traditions. Instead of finding release and joy, however, they are frustrated and tired

of the journey. They have a sense of hopelessness and helplessness. Theirs has been a labor without reward.

But Jesus offers them an alternative. They can exchange the heavy yoke of the law and traditions which they have accepted as the way to God for another yoke, a different yoke. It is the yoke of discipleship rather than a yoke of the law. They are invited to learn from the one who is "gentle and lowly in heart." His life is characterized by complete, trustful dependence on God. By entering into his way, men will find rest for their souls, that is, a joyous, renewing relationship with God.

This is the reason why his "yoke is easy and his burden is light." It is not that the way of discipleship is a permissive, unrestrained, immoral, and unethical approach. It is not that Jesus asks less in the way of personal goodness and responsibility to God and man. Not at all. The opposite is true. He asks more in terms of personal goodness, as we saw in the Sermon on the Mount.

"Rest for your souls" is not to be equated with idleness or lack of purpose and commitment. Rather, Jesus is asking people to give up their own striving in an attempt to wrest salvation from God and join him in humble dependence upon the Father. When they do this, they will find incredibly that God is there in their lives and that he will make life joyous, zestful, and creative, instead of wearisome and frustrated.

10.
An Evil Generation

12:1-50

I. Controversies over the Sabbath (12:1-21)

Jesus responds to the Pharisees who criticize his disciples for gathering grain to eat on the sabbath. Later he heals a crippled man, thereby breaking the sabbath traditions. This enrages the Pharisees who make plans to kill him.

1. The disciples violate the sabbath traditions. By custom, travellers in Palestine were allowed to help themselves to the fruit of the fields through which they passed to satisfy hunger. So the disciples were not stealing when they took grains of barley to eat. However, they were breaking two of the thirty-nine proscriptions against work on the sabbath contained in the oral law. By plucking the grain, they were reaping. When they rubbed the husks off it in order to eat it, they were threshing. These activities created resentment among the Pharisees who were characterized by their devotion to the oral traditions.

Jesus countered the criticisms of the Pharisees by citing two examples from the Old Testament and by quoting a passage from Hosea. In the first example, David broke the law when he and his men ate the "bread of the presence" (1 Sam. 21:1-6). The bread of the presence was the twelve loaves baked on Friday and placed each sabbath before the Lord in the Temple (Ex. 25:30; Lev. 24:5). When it was replaced, it was to be eaten by the priests (Lev. 24:9). But under the pressure of hunger, David demanded this holy bread from Ahimelech, the priest, and it was eaten by him and his men.

The point in the illustration is that human necessity takes precedence over religious ritual. This seems to have been a guiding principle in the ministry of Jesus. People were more important than religious institutions and ritual. This caused Jesus to reject a wooden, literalistic interpretation of the law. His was a spontaneous, dynamic approach to religion which caused him to relate realistically to situations in life. Human welfare took precedence over all other considerations.

In the second example, Jesus pointed out that the priests themselves were guilty of violating the law. The same law which forbad work on the sabbath also commanded the priests to offer sabbath sacrifices (Num. 28:9-10). This presented a real problem to the Jewish scholars. Which is more important: the law against work on the sabbath or the law commanding sabbath sacrifices which could not be offered if the priests did not work? They concluded that the sacrificial service in the Temple was more important.

But Jesus reminded his hearers that "something greater than the temple" was in their midst. That something was Jesus and his work. The disciples were in a service holier and higher than the service of the Temple. They were priests of God in a new age, and in that service they could also break the law against sabbath labor.

Finally, Jesus cited a passage from Hosea 6:6 which set forth his guiding principle: "I desire mercy and not sacrifice." The problem with people who were slaves to religious tradition was their lovelessness. They thought that they would please God by the punctilious performance of religious duties. But anyone who tries to serve God in this way is going to miss out on God's real demand upon his life. Blind subservience to ritual will sooner or later lead to a callous disregard for human need.

The Lord must experience a great disappointment with his followers who so often fall into the same kind of sin as the Pharisees. The perennial danger of religion is that the welfare of its institutions will be elevated above that of people. How many people have been coldly and self-righteously thrust aside or even crushed because they did not fit into the program of a church or organization? And this in service to institutions presumably created to honor and serve Jesus himself!

Jesus concluded his remarks with the bold declaration: "The Son of man is lord of the sabbath." He assumed the prerogative of ordering the lives of his disciples. He could determine the meaning of the sabbath in the new age that was dawning in their midst. Among other things, this surely means that we cannot determine the will of God for believers by a literalistic interpretation and application of the teachings of the Old Testament. Everything must be judged in the light of the decisive revelation that God has given us in his Son.

2. Jesus heals a man on the sabbath. The incident about the man with the withered hand shows the stark contrast between Jesus' attitude toward people and that of the religious leaders. They cared nothing about the man. He was only important to them insofar as they could use him to further their own schemes.

The presence of the man gave them an excuse to bait Jesus with a question: "Is it lawful to heal on the sabbath?" To this question the theologians gave a qualified answer. It was lawful to violate the sabbath traditions to help a person whose life was in immediate danger. But the man with the withered hand obviously did not fall into that category. It was certainly a small thing to wait until sundown, when the sabbath ended, in order to heal the man.

But Jesus reminded them that their own traditions allowed them to rescue an animal who had fallen into a pit on the sabbath. A man was of far more value than a sheep. At least, Jesus put human beings above animals in his scale of values. Many people, however, do not. Our society, which spends more on food for pets than on food for the hungry, evidently contains many people who consider animals to be of more worth than human beings.

Thereupon, Jesus enunciated his own view of the sabbath. It

is lawful to do good on the sabbath. He took a positive rather than a negative approach to the day. He did not believe that any helpful, constructive act designed to relieve human misery was out of place on the sabbath. In fact, he believed that it was wrong not to do such a deed. And so he healed the man.

3. The anger of the Pharisees. According to Matthew, this miracle so infuriated the Pharisees that they began to plot to kill Jesus. He constituted such a threat to their beloved traditions that they could no longer tolerate him. Probably the reason for their fury was the fact that their own power and prestige were tied to the elaborately constructed oral traditions. Their scribes were the renowned theologians whose interpretations about what was lawful or unlawful were widely sought and respected. The Pharisees themselves were honored as godly examples of the highest piety because they so scrupulously kept those traditions. If unchecked, Jesus with his revolutionary ideas would bring all that to an end.

When people furiously defend an institution, one must always ask the question: Is it because the institution is so important and necessary? Or, is it because their own future and position in society depend upon maintaining it? Many religious institutions and programs have long outlived their usefulness, because they were defended by people whose personal welfare was tied to their continued existence.

4. The servant of the Lord. Matthew believed that Jesus, whom the Pharisees rejected, was none other than the servant of the Lord about whom Isaiah had spoken (Isa. 42:1-4). The passage delineates characteristics of the servant which Matthew detected in the ministry of Jesus. His gospel was of universal significance; it was intended for Gentiles as well as Jews. He attempted to avoid the sensationalism which his mighty deeds tended to create. He was tender and compassionate with bruised and hurt people; he did not "break a bruised reed or quench a smoldering wick." Nevertheless, this tender, unselfish servant of God would bring about the triumph of justice.

II. The Sin Against the Spirit (Matt. 12:22-37)

His enemies claim that Jesus' healing power comes from Beelzebul, prince of the devils. He points out the fallacies in that claim and accuses them of blasphemy against the Spirit. Their words, which proceed from an evil heart, will have to be accounted for on the day of judgment.

1. Son of David or servant of Beelzebul? Jesus healed a mute which prompted the people to ask: "Can this be the son of David?" This, of course, was the correct assumption. Jesus' works were the sign of his messianic authority.

But the Pharisees countered with an assertion which pointed in exactly the opposite direction. They said that his power came from Beelzebul, prince of the devils. That is, his authority was from Satan. Beelzebul, meaning "Lord of the temple," was the god of Ekron (2 Kings 1:2). In a sarcastic play on the name the Jews often called him Beelzebub, "lord of the flies."

Jesus countered the assertion with two arguments. First, he showed that it was illogical. Satan would hardly use his power against demons, the forces that served him. This would indicate that there was civil war among the powers of evil. Second, Jesus showed that the accusation was arbitrary. When the Pharisees performed the same kind of miracles, they did not attribute them to Satan. "Your sons" means people who belong to your circle. There was no basis for attributing the Pharisees' casting out of demons to God while at the same time saying that Jesus was acting as a servant of the devil when he did exactly the same thing. The only explanation for their irrational arbitrariness was their personal animosity toward Jesus.

Then Jesus declared the true meaning of the miracles. They were a revelation of the presence of God's kingdom (rule) in his own person.

2. Blasphemy against the Holy Spirit. The Pharisees had

committed a terrible and dangerous sin. They had attributed the work of God to the devil. For this sin, declared Jesus, there is no forgiveness.

People have held a number of false and even destructive ideas about the sin against the Holy Spirit. It is not a direct attack on God. It is not even cursing God. As Jesus said, it was not even a personal criticism against him. Moreover, it is not the kind of sin that can be committed in ignorance. It must be willful and perverse. God reveals himself, and the individual knows in his heart that he has received a revelation from God. But instead of acknowledging God's revelation for what it is, he perversely attributes it to evil. In other words, he turns theology upside down; God becomes the devil, and the devil becomes God.

Jesus declared that this sin is unforgivable. The reason for this is very obvious. If we willfully declare that God's redemptive revelation to us really comes from the devil, there is then no way that God can reach us. The Pharisees, having deliberately closed their eyes to God's most crucial revelation of himself to them, were outside the pale. There was no hope for them—so long as they continued in this evil, stubborn resistance to God. But this does not mean that even they could not change their attitude and repent, receiving God's saving revelation to them for what it was. To say that the sin against the Spirit is unforgiveable is not to say that the persons who commit it cannot be forgiven and saved if they change their stubborn opposition to God.

3. The tree and its fruit. We have already encountered an illustration about trees and fruit in another context (Matt. 7:17). In the present passage, Jesus seems to have used it to say that the Pharisees' criticisms are simply an evidence of the true quality of their lives. They were incoherent in their criticism of him. Healing a mute was a good act from any point of view. But that good fruit, they had said, proceeded from an evil source. This was a contradiction. They needed either to "make the tree good, and its fruit good; or make the tree bad, and its fruit bad."

There was, however, no contradiction between their deeds and their evil nature. Their words were evil because they proceeded out of a corrupt interior.

Jesus asserted that they would be held accountable for the charges they had made, for "on the day of judgment men will render account for every careless word they utter." Their own words would be the evidence against them. By this evidence they would be "justified," that is, pronounced innocent. The term justified is basically a legal one. Their words also could furnish the basis for a guilty verdict in God's great court.

III. The Demand for a Sign (Matt. 12:38-50)

Jesus rejects the demand of the scribes and Pharisees for a sign. They will indeed receive a sign, but not the one they desire. It will be Jesus' death and resurrection. He tells a story of a man possessed again by demons to illustrate the danger facing his stubborn hearers who have not allowed their empty lives to be filled by God. Finally, he refuses to acknowledge the claim of his physical relatives, stressing his deeper relationship with his new family, the people of God.

1. The sign of Jonah.   The demand for a sign was not unusual. Religious leaders and teachers who claimed to have a special mission were expected to validate their claim with a sign. Whether the request was sincere or hypocritical we do not know. Would the scribes and Pharisees have believed had Jesus acceded to their demand?

At any rate, the Gospels consistently show that Jesus did not produce signs upon demand. He acted in sovereign freedom in accordance with his own concept of his ministry. Moreover, the Gospels also show that Jesus did not wish to be accepted as a sensational miracle-worker. He knew that faith produced by miracles is superficial at best.

The crucial sign to his generation would be the sign of his

death and resurrection to which Jonah's experience was analagous. Jonah had spent three days in the whale after which God had delivered him. Jesus would spend three days in the earth (dead and buried) from which he would emerge, resurrected by God's power. According to the Gospel story, Jesus spent only one full day in the tomb. But in Jewish reckoning any part of a day was counted as a day.

The problem with the religious leaders was their perverse blindness, their insincerity, their willful refusal to acknowledge the presence of God's rule among them in the person of Jesus. This stubborn rejection of Jesus is all the more serious when compared to the people of Nineveh and to the queen of the South. Nineveh had repented at the preaching of Jonah. The queen of the South had given enough credence to the stories reaching her kingdom about Solomon's greatness that she made a long journey to verify their authenticity personally. Something greater than either Jonah or Solomon was present among the Jewish leaders. That something was the rule of God expressing itself in the words and deeds of Jesus. But the scribes and Pharisees, confronted with the presence of God in a way much more compelling than his revelation to those people in an earlier time, had shown no such sincerity and openness to his actions in their midst. In the judgment they might claim not to have had sufficient evidence on which to base an adequate response. But all God would have to do would be to point to the people of Nineveh and the famed queen. They had responded with far less evidence.

2. Empty houses.   The story told by Jesus about unclean spirits (demons) reflects the views on demonology current in his day. A demon, exorcised from a man, wanders in a waterless place (a desert). The desert was thought to be a region appropriate to homeless demons. There he associates himself with seven other demons. Seeking to find another home, the demon returns with his fellows to find that the man in whom he had once dwelled is still susceptible to demon possession. Nothing had entered to occupy the space left by the departed spirit.

The story seems to be applied to Jesus' opponents. They are interested in cleaning up their lives. But they have failed to allow them to be filled by God's presence, since they have rejected Jesus. The problem with legalism is its negative approach to religion. It attempts to eliminate impurities from the life, but it does not fill that life with the Spirit of God. No matter how successful the program of legalism may be in ridding the life of evil, it cannot deal with the problem of emptiness. The purpose of Jesus, the Messiah, was to fill empty lives with God's spirit. Thus garrisoned, the life is capable of resisting the onslaught of evil.

11.
Secrets of the Kingdom
13:1-58

According to the Synoptic Gospels, the parable was a major form used by Jesus in his teaching. He was not the inventor of the parable, but no one ever used it more masterfully than he. For centuries Jesus' parables were usually understood as allegories. This kind of interpretation often led to wild and foolish conclusions. Everything was thought to have meaning, which might be related to the times or to the interpreter. Some of Jesus' stories do indeed demand an allegorical interpretation, but it should be used with much care. Usually the parables have one major point, and the primary responsibility of the interpreter is to isolate and understand that one point.

Seven parables, generally called parables of the kingdom, are found in Matthew 13. Grouping materials in this way is characteristic of Matthew's Gospel, as we have seen. These parables constitute the sayings section of the third major division in Matthew, which ends with the characteristic statement found in Matthew 13:53. In our consideration of these parables, we shall group them according to their major points—the problem, question, or truth to which they seem to be directed.

The introduction to these parables in our English versions is somewhat misleading. Jesus did not mean that the kingdom is like a treasure, a pearl, a net, or any of the other objects mentioned in the stories. He meant that the situation described in the parables gives some insight into a truth about the kingdom or reign of God.

I. The Problem of Varied Responses to the Gospel (Matt. 13:1-23)

Jesus tells the parable of the soils to a multitude assembled at the seashore. He explains to the disciples the reason for his teaching in parables. They are vehicles both of enlightenment and of mystery. He then explains the parable to the disciples.

1. The problem.   Our parable speaks to a crucial and universal problem. In terms of Jesus' ministry it may be stated thus: Why did more people not respond positively to his preaching, if he was indeed Israel's Messiah? This question was probably raised by the disciples many times. The danger which accompanies this question is that a lack of response may dampen the enthusiasm of the believer and cause him to doubt the efficacy of the gospel.

This is a continuing problem for Christians. We tend to be influenced by statistics. If something is not widely accepted, we are prone to question its validity. There has never been a time when this was more true than in our day, equipped as we are to gather data and measure results statistically. We fall into the trap of believing that God's blessings can be measured in terms of the number of people who respond.

2. The answer.   The parable is often called the parable of the sower. But this directs the attention to the wrong aspect of it. It is really the parable of the soils. Jesus says that the variety of responses is determined by the way that different hearers receive the word. But his major point is contained in the conclusion of the parable. The harvest is assured, for God guarantees it. Some of the seed will fall into good soil, producing an abundant harvest. The disciples can face the future with confidence, therefore, undismayed by negative and lukewarm responses. God's redemptive purposes will ultimately be achieved.

3. Why teach in parables?   The answer given to this question in 13:13 is somewhat disturbing. For one thing, a parable is intended to clarify and not to obscure. It is an illustration of divine truth couched in a common, everyday experience accessible to anyone. Moreover, we cannot believe that Jesus deliberately desired to exclude anyone or that God himself is responsible for human rebellion against the message of redemption.

We should recognize, however, that God himself chose a particular way of redeeming man. Theoretically, he could have gone about it in some other way, indeed, in any way that he chose to do it. He decided that he would not use a method of redemption open only to the wise or to any other elite segment of society. His redemption is not given as a reward for virtue or work. Redemption is not a prize given to the educated and intelligent because of their superior knowledge. Redemption is a gift that must be received humbly and gratefully. In order to be redeemed a person needs to turn to God in childlike dependence and openness to his message. Indeed, the simplicity of the gospel is its greatest stumbling block for many people, especially to those who depend upon their own efforts or wisdom.

God wants to save all men. But he has chosen a method that necessarily excludes many. Jesus wanted all Israel to repent. But the way he came to them, as a carpenter's son, and the way he spoke to them, in parables and otherwise, meant that many would reject him. His way was an affront to their logic and pride. This is the inevitable consequence of God's plan of redemption, but not the result of his desire to condemn anyone.

"Him who has" (v. 12) refers specifically to the person who is open and receptive to God's revelation to him. The possibility of an increasing perception of God's truth and of an increasing appropriation of God's blessings is his. "More will be given" to him.

In contrast to the Israelites of whom Isaiah spoke (quoted in vv. 14-15) and to the rebellious people of Jesus' own day, the disciples had the capacity to hear and to see. They were open to what God was doing in their midst. Because of this responsiveness, they had the incredible privilege of witnessing the unveiling of God's salvation which God's prophets and other servants had hoped to see in their own day.

4. The parable explained. The explanation of the parable shows us what it meant to Christians to whom Matthew was writing and what it means to us today. It divides the hearers of the gospel into four classes, using an illustration drawn from well-known agricultural experiences. The four kinds of responses correspond to the types of soil with which the Palestinian farmer had to contend in his struggle to raise a crop.

At the time for planting, the farmer scattered the seed broadcast in his field and subsequently turned them under with his primitive plow. Consequently the seed fell indiscriminately on different kinds of soil. The farmer knew this, but he sowed with the confidence that some of the seed would fall on good soil. He firmly expected that the harvest would be great enough to compensate for the seed that failed to produce. Jesus taught that the sower of the gospel was in the same situation.

The path was the hardened trail hammered out by the feet of people who had been passing through the farmer's field since the last harvest. Seed falling on it were particularly vulnerable to the rapacious birds, the farmer's special enemy at the time of sowing. This soil represents the hardened, callous hearer who is unreceptive to the word of salvation. His hardness may be the result of his own self-righteousness, of his evil perversity, or of his pride in his own wisdom. The way God has acted does not seem to fit into his logical presupposition of the way God must act. So he hardens his heart and resists God's action.

The rocky ground describes the places where thin soil covers an underlying layer of sandstone which now and again comes to the surface. The seed sown there springs up quickly and the plants look promising. But the promise is deceptive, for it soon succumbs to the withering heat of the sun. This soil represents those who often respond enthusiastically but superficially to the gospel. They have not counted the cost. They do not understand that following Jesus is difficult. And when difficulties arise, they drop out.

The Palestinian farmer had to contend with a variety of weeds, some of which bore nettles or thorns. Plants growing from seed sown in soil infested with thorns could not contend with their competitors. The thorns, growing more rapidly than the young plants, robbed them of their space and nutrients and choked them out. The seed of the gospel in like manner often has to contend with competing ambitions and desires in the life of many people. "The cares of the world and delight in riches" do indeed "choke the word" so that it does not produce the desired harvest.

But some of the seed does fall in good soil and produces an abundant harvest. Jesus used exaggerated figures. No Palestinian farmer expected a yield of a hundredfold. But we must remember that Jesus was illustrating truth about the kingdom in his parable. While the figures may have been exaggerated in terms of the harvest expected by the farmer, they were not exaggerated in terms of the kingdom. The harvest that God will bring about will exceed by far the most optimistic dreams of the sower.

II. The Problem of Authenticity (Matt. 13:24-30,36-43, 47-50)

Jesus warns his disciples against trying to separate genuine disciples from false ones. He gives this warning in two parables. The first is about the weeds growing in a field of wheat (Matt. 13:24-30). An interpretation of the parable is given in verses 36-43. The parable of the net teaches the same lesson (Matt. 13:47-50).

1. The problem. From the very beginning believers knew that some of the professed followers of Jesus were counterfeit. This problem is illustrated in the experiences of the twelve. Even one of those chosen by Jesus to form the nucleus of the new Israel was a traitor.

This continues to be a problem for the church today. How can we distinguish a sincere Christian from the insincere one? There is another related question: What is the responsibility of the church in "weeding-out" false Christians?

Sometimes these questions are raised because of an unchristian and sinful attitude. There are always church members who are arrogant about their own status. They think of themselves as representatives of the highest and best in Christian profession and practice. They are the "spiritual ones," ever concerned about "unspiritual" church members. They feel that God has given them the responsibility of eliminating the "heretics" from the body!

But the questions are raised also by good Christians out of real concern for the church and its witness. Sincere Christians want the church to be better. They are dismayed by attitudes and acts which jeopardize the witness of the church to the unchristian world. They feel a personal responsibility for the purity of the church and are frustrated by the sin and indifference apparent in the lives of many of its members. The parables under consideration speak, therefore, to a very serious problem and what is often a very genuine concern.

2. *The parable of the weeds.* Jesus said that the situation of the kingdom was much like that of a man who sowed good seeds of wheat in his field. After this, however, a man bent on doing him harm sowed weeds in the field. After the seeds, both good and bad, had sprouted, the man's laborers detected what had been done. They came to him with a suggested solution. Shall we, they asked, go into the field and pull up the weeds?

The owner felt, however, that the solution was worse than the problem. The difficulty lay in the fact that these particular weeds, bearded darnel, looked very much like the wheat itself. His men might not be able to distinguish between the weeds and the wheat and thus probably would destroy the good plants in their efforts to get rid of the bad.

He felt that the harvest would be a more appropriate time

to deal with the problem of the weeds. Then they would be easily distinguished from the wheat. At that time his servants could safely go into the fields, gather the weeds, and burn them. Afterward they could gather the grain and store it into the barn.

3. *The lesson of the parable.* In the interpretation of the parable (vv. 36-43), it is clear that Jesus is talking about people rather than wheat and weeds. The wheat are the sons of the kingdom; the weeds are the sons of the evil one.

The position of Jesus is clear. His followers are to make no premature attempt to weed out false disciples from true ones. Two reasons for this arise from the parable.

In the first instance, disciples do not have the capacity to do the job. They cannot distinguish clearly between true and false believers any more than the laborers could distinguish between weeds and wheat. In Matthew, Jesus has already spoken to this point when he said: "Judge not, that you be not judged" (7:1). The comments made at that point apply also here. Judgment in an ultimate sense does not belong to men, even saved men. That is a prerogative which God reserves for himself alone.

Every once in a while we hear someone make this kind of remark about another person: "I do not believe he is saved." This is exactly the kind of judgment which Jesus in his teaching forbids us to make. We can say perhaps: "He is not living a Christian life." We can observe the presence of sin in the life of another person. But we can never say that he is not a son of the kingdom. We just do not know enough to be able to say that.

In the second place, Jesus teaches that there is a time appointed by God when a genuine separation will be made. It is the time of the harvest. The interpretation of the parable says that this will come at the "close of the age" (v. 40). It also says that God through his own chosen instruments will make that separation. This is not a responsibility of believers either now or in the future.

This is truly a liberating concept. The believer does not have to bear the responsibility for judging others. He can have faith that God will act appropriately in his own time. The believer can spend his energy in living the Christian life, preaching the gospel, and ministering to others with the knowledge that God, and God alone, both saves and judges.

4. *The parable of the net.* This is a twin to the parable of the weeds, teaching exactly the same lesson. The net which is cast into the sea is a seine. It could be pulled between two boats, or it could be cast out from a boat and pulled to the shore by means of ropes.

Anyone who has seined for fish or who has watched fishermen working their nets is familiar with the picture in the parable. All kinds of fish and marine life are picked up by the seine. When it is drawn ashore or pulled up on the fishing boat, the fishermen have the job of sorting out their catch. There are edible and inedible fish. The "bad" fish to the Jewish fisherman were any that did not have scales or fins.

Jesus was a realist. He knew that when the net of the gospel was cast out, it would enclose both good and bad, that is, true and false, disciples. This is inevitable, and so it should not alarm us.

Our concern should not be with sorting out the catch. Rather, we should be concerned that we preach the gospel in such a way that we do not encourage false professions of faith. It is our job to put out the net. It is God's responsibility to sort out the catch.

III. The Problem of Small Beginnings (Matt. 13:31-33)

Jesus compares the kingdom to what happens when a mustard seed is planted. It produces a large plant. He also compares it to the effect of leaven which permeates a huge quantity of meal (flour).

1. *The problem.* People are generally impressed by size. They equate power and influence with bigness. This was a problem

at the very beginning of the Christian movement. Jewish people expected God to bring in his kingdom with an awesome display of grandeur and power. The disciples, no doubt, shared these common concepts of the messianic age.

How were they to harmonize what was actually happening with their traditional ideas? God was not in fact revealing himself in overwhelming power. Only a small minority of the Jewish people had been attracted to Jesus. Most of these were from the lower strata of Jewish life. Even his closest associates, the twelve, were former fishermen, tax collectors, and the like. The power structure of the Jewish nation, not to mention that of the Roman Empire, was unchanged by what Jesus was doing.

2. The answer. Jesus told the two parables to show that commonly held ideas in which power is associated with bigness and status with ostentatious display were mistaken when applied to the kingdom.

The kingdom, rather, is to be compared to what happens to a mustard seed. It is extremely small. One would hardly guess its real potential by looking at its size. But when it is sown, it sprouts into such a huge plant that it could be called a tree. The plants about which Jesus spoke attained a height of eight to ten feet in Palestine.

Some interpreters have seen in one aspect of Jesus' parable a prediction of the universality of the gospel. The birds which make their home in the plant are symbolic of the Gentiles who will be included in the kingdom as the gospel is preached in the world (see Ezek. 17:3; 31:6; Dan. 4:12). This may be a correct interpretation, but it is not the central point of the parable.

The parable expresses Jesus' joyous confidence in the kingdom. God has manifested his kingdom in such a small way, in the ministry of an obscure Galilean in an insignificant place in the world, far from the centers of power. But Jesus had no doubt about the future of the kingdom. He believed that these small beginnings would eventuate in the triumph of God's rule.

His confidence was not based on statistics. Instead, his optimism arose from his undaunted faith in God's purposes and power. God would bring to fruition what he had begun.

When we are surrounded by crowds and taste the heady wine of success, it is easy to believe in the future of the gospel. But the real test comes at the moment when outward circumstances do not give us cause for confidence. Do we believe then in the certain triumph of the rule of God?

The parable of the leaven illustrates another aspect of the kingdom. Once again there is a contrast with the smallness of the leaven and the quantity of the flour. Three measures of meal would produce enough bread to feed about 160 persons.

But there is an additional idea. The leaven works quietly and mysteriously as it permeates the dough. Contrary to popular belief, God had not chosen to manifest his rule in spectacular, overpowering ways. He had chosen instead to work in unobtrusive, even hidden ways.

He could have unleashed his mighty power against the forces of evil and brought about a devastating coup. But he had refused that approach. His kingdom would be as leaven in the world. It would spread from life to life, changing and transforming men and women one by one. This method of the kingdom is gradual and slow. It produces impatience, irritation, and even skepticism and unbelief. Why would not an all-powerful God use all the resources at his command? That is hard to understand, given our own presuppositions. If we had his power, we would not follow the path God followed. But Jesus recognized God's way. He chose to follow it at great price. There were people who would gladly have followed him in a mighty messianic war of conquest. But these same people cried for his blood when he failed to perform in the way they thought God should act.

IV. The Worth of the Kingdom (Matt. 13:44-46)

Jesus compares the kingdom to the situation of two men. One discovers a treasure hidden in a field and the other finds a valuable pearl. In both instances the men sell all they have to purchase the valuables they discover, because they wisely have recognized their worth. As a conclusion to this group of parables, Jesus compares the man trained for the kingdom to a person of means who brings out of his treasures what is new and old.

1. The parables.   The two parables, one about treasure hidden in a field and the other about a very valuable pearl, emphasize the surpassing worth of the kingdom. But the major point probably is the reaction of the men in the light of their discovery.

It is said of the first that he was filled with great joy when he discovered the treasure hidden in the field. The same no doubt can be inferred about the man who found the unusual pearl. So filled are they with the desire to possess these newly found treasures that they gladly part with everything they have to raise the money to buy them.

Such is the case with the person who discovers the value of the kingdom. The discovery will cause him to know that he cannot live without it, and he will do anything at all to make it his own. He will gladly give up all he has to possess it.

In their interpretation of these two short parables, many people have understood its central teaching to be the cost of the kingdom. One cannot possess it unless he is willing to give up all else. This implication is found in them, and it is certainly in keeping with many other passages found in the New Testament. But it is not the central idea.

In the two stories neither man feels that he is making a sacrifice. In each case the prize desired is seen to be worth much more than the wealth they already possess. They give up everything they own willingly and gladly.

This leads us inevitably to raise a question. Why does our attitude not correspond more to the attitude of the men in Jesus' stories? Why are we so grudging in our approach to Christian service? Why are we so complaining and fretful if we feel that we have to make some small sacrifice for the cause of Christ?

The answer is perhaps the obvious one. We do not really believe in the surpassing worth of the kingdom. We do not truly believe that being a child of God and living under his rule is the most worthwhile possession of all. For the most part we have not been overwhelmed by our discovery of the riches made available to us through the gospel.

2. The ideal disciple. Many scholars have suggested that verse 52 may represent a self-portrait of the author of this Gospel. He was a scribe, a person who had been trained in the Jewish law and who had become a legal expert. But he had heard the gospel and had seen it as a fulfillment of the Judaism in which he had been reared. This is, as you can see, only a guess. It may be true, but it may also be wide of the mark.

At any rate, the meaning of the statement is clear. The person "trained for the kingdom" is one who is not only a disciple but who has studied and grown mature in his understanding of the gospel. This mature kind of Christian leader or ideal disciple is one who has been able to relate the revelation of God in the Old Testament to the new revelation in the gospel.

He does not reject the old. He recognizes the validity of what God has done in the past. But he also does not reject the new. He sees the worth of both and perceives the continuity of God's activity through the ages, culminating in the climactic revelation of himself in Jesus of Nazareth.

V. The Return Home (Matt. 13:53-58)

Jesus returns to his own country (Nazareth) where he teaches in the synagogue. The people are astonished at his wisdom. They reject him, however, because they know him and his family.

1. The right question. The center of Jesus' ministry in Galilee was Capernaum. The Gospels give no hint as to why Jesus made this choice. In the course of his ministry he returned to Nazareth where, as was often his custom, he taught in the synagogue—that is, he delivered the lecture or sermon during the synagogue service.

He must have spoken there, as we know he did in other occasions, without quoting the wisdom of the rabbis. The people could not account for the insight and depth of his teachings. They had never heard anybody say what he was saying. Where did he get such wisdom? This was the appropriate question. Had they followed it to its logical conclusion, they would have found the answer: his direct, unmediated wisdom came from God and was due to his special relation with God.

2. The rejection. The people, however, refused to seek the answer to the question. This man could not be anyone special. They knew him and his whole family.

Ah, that is the error. They thought they knew him! But they did not. They could not penetrate beneath the veil of the incarnation. They followed their own logic and, as a result, rejected the word of God.

They expected God to act through someone special—certainly not through a hometown boy. A major lesson of the incarnation is that God acts in surprising unexpected ways. He enters the world through the birth of a baby in a manger. Now, who could have imagined that? Of one thing we can be sure. The person who thinks he has God all figured out is inevitably going to be mistaken and be blind to what he actually does.